160+ WRITE AND

SIGHT WORDS

PRACTICE PAGES

about

swims

wait

could

above

anyone

children

usually

done

beautiful

afraind

clock

before

hard

think

Books made by **Brain Hunter Prep**
with love from **New York**

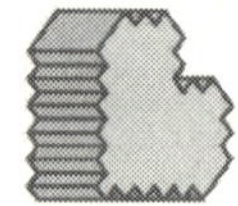

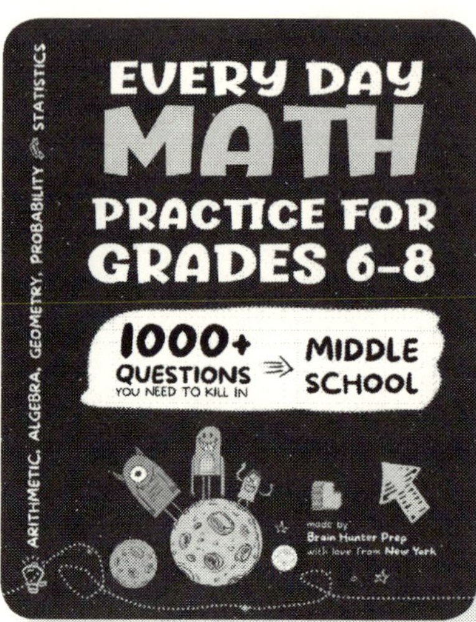

more coming soon

Want an amazing offer from Brain Hunter?

800+ MATH

practice questions absolutely for free

Leave us a review on Amazon and contact us back at:

info@brainhunterprep.com
and we will email you printable PDF worksheets.

ISBN: 978-1946755339
Published by Brain Hunter Prep, Inc.

Aknowlegments:
Icons made by Freepik, Smashicons, Nikita Golubev Pixel Buddha, Good Ware, Pause08, mynamepong, DinosoftLabs, Vectors Market,turkkub, Those Icons Nikita Golubev, Roundicons, Twitter from www.flaticon.com

SIGHT WORDS COVERED

1. What is this story **about**?
2. My uncle lives **above** me.
3. **After** playing sports, I make sure to drink water.
4. It's raining **again**!
5. We are **almost** there.
6. My mom is looking for **another** job.
7. We **are** from Europe.
8. Kim wants to travel **around** the world.
9. Roses are **beautiful**.
10. I am a good student **because** I study.
11. I brush my teeth **before** bedtime.
12. I don't like **being** late.
13. Mary is the **best** student in the class.
14. She is wearing **black** socks.
15. I have three **brothers** and one sister.
16. My friend is afraid of **bugs**.
17. Mike's shirt is **blue**.
18. There are twelve **children** in the class.
19. The **clock** stopped working.
20. Do you know the seven **colors** in a rainbow?
21. **Could** I use your desk?
22. **Didn't** you come to the party yesterday?
23. We **don't** have any sugar left.
24. I am almost **done** with my homework.
25. **Does** Julia play the piano?
26. They admire **each** other.
27. A stop sign has **eight** sides.
28. I like to **eat** apples.
29. How does the story **end**?
30. Where can I **find** toothpaste?
31. This is my **first** time in Japan.
32. The traffic light is **green**.
33. Jill is a very **hard** worker.
34. Did you **hear** that?
35. I accidently fell and **hurt** my knee.
36. **It's** always sunny in Philadelphia.
37. The train **just** left.
38. Do you **know** her name?
39. My dad works for a **large** company.
40. I am **never** late to school.
41. My teacher retires **next** year.
42. I go to the dentist **once** a year.
43. Banks **open** at eight o'clock.
44. Is that a cat **or** a dog?
45. John and Lucy are married to each **other**.
46. Welcome to **our** home.
47. Matt **put** his luggage down.
48. Slow and steady wins the **race**.
49. Is it going to **rain** tomorrow?
50. I like to **read** books everyday.
51. I **really** like playing basketball.
52. The earth is **round**.
53. Christmas is coming **soon**.
54. Julia is my **second** cousin.
55. I drank **seven** glasses of water today.
56. It will soon be **spring**.
57. Can you read me a bedtime **story**?
58. Why is everyone in **such** a hurry?

SIGHT WORDS COVERED

59. Be **sure** to eat your vegetables everyday!
60. That's a beautiful dress.
61. How old do you **think** I am?
62. Those are my books.
63. We had a really good **time**.
64. Is it going to rain **today**?
65. My friend and I go to school **together**.
66. This box is **too** heavy.
67. Don't forget to **turn** off the light.
68. The **train** is now arriving.
69. Lisa has **two** dogs and one cat.
70. I **usually** walk to school.
71. I can't **wait** to go on vacation.
72. I **wish** I had a room of my own.
73. He **won** first place in the science fair.
74. The car engine does not **work**.
75. Would you care to go to the zoo?
76. The **wind** grew stronger
77. Come eat **with** us!
78. I am **writing** a letter to my aunt.
79. Chris went to Spain last **year**.
80. Bananas are **yellow**.
81. Tom is **afraid** of spiders.
82. We **almost** won the soccer game.
83. Do you **also** like jazz?
84. I **always** try my best.
85. What is your favorite **animal**?
86. Can **anyone** help me?
87. My dad will be **away** for a week.
88. Mary wants to **become** a doctor.
89. Always **believe** in yourself!
90. He **swims** better than I do.
91. Let's **build** a snowman!
92. Lisa wants to **buy** a new car.
93. I don't **care** for eggs.
94. We **caught** a big fish on our trip.
95. I need to wash my **clothes**.
96. Luis is an activist in his **community**.
97. What **country** were you born in?
98. We **decided** to go see a movie.
99. Can we watch a **different** TV show?
100. The scientist **discovered** a new comet.
101. Does this book belong to you?
102. I am almost **done** eating.
103. He didn't run fast **enough** to catch the bus.
104. This book is designed **especially** for students.
105. I love to make **everybody** happy.
106. My father works every day **except** Sunday.
107. I **finally** beat Mark at chess.
108. That cat is very **friendly**!
109. I **generally** walk to school.
110. It was **getting** late.
111. We studied **hard** and passed the test.
112. I **heard** the birds singing.
113. The moon was **hidden** behind the clouds.
114. My dog dug a **hole** in the garden.
115. This exam is very **important**.
116. It's **impossible** to climb that mountain!
117. Lisa is a strong, **independent** woman.
118. The flag is on **its** pole.

SIGHT WORDS COVERED

119. I write in my **journal** often.
120. He **knew** what he wanted for his birthday.
121. I don't **know** her name.
122. Everybody **laughed** a great deal.
123. I accidently **left** my bag in school.
124. I **live** in New York City.
125. She is a very **lovable** person.
126. I'm going to need some **money**.
127. I take a shower in the **morning** before school.
128. I built this treehouse by **myself**!
129. We should **never** give up on our dreams.
130. How was your **night**?
131. Luis went to the gym **once** a week.
132. Would you like to play **outside**?
133. My parents **own** their house.
134. Dinner is **probably** ready by now.
135. How do you solve this **problem**?
136. May I ask a **question**?
137. Ashley is getting **ready** to leave the house.
138. Do you **recycle**?
139. We all have important **responsibilities**.
140. You **shouldn't** exercise on a full stomach.
141. Is **something** missing from here?
142. All of a **sudden**, a fire broke out!
143. Are you **sure** you want to do this?
144. We thought the movie was **terrible**.
145. I hope she is not in **trouble**.
146. **These** flowers are beautiful.
147. Jim **threw** the ball to Dave.
148. I glanced **through** the brochure.
149. My teacher **told** me I should study.
150. I don't have class **until** 9 o'clock.
151. I can't wait for summer **vacation**.
152. Please **watch** your step.
153. What are you going to **wear** to the party?
154. The **weather** is looking great all week!
155. **Which** subject do you like best?
156. I fell asleep **while** reading a book.
157. We spent the **whole** day fishing.
158. We went to China last **year**.
159. May I borrow **your** book?
160. Are you sure **you're** alright?

Sight Words you need to know

LET'S BEGIN OUR JOURNEY TO RECOGNIZE AND LEARN SIGHT WORDS.

What is this story **about**?

Trace the word:

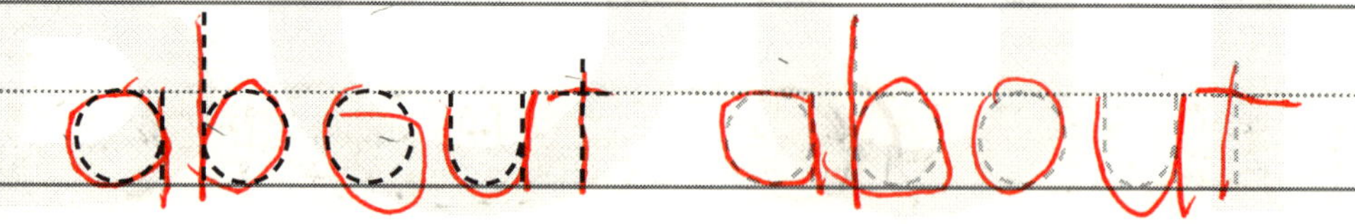

Write the word:

Color the pizza slices that have the word "**about**"

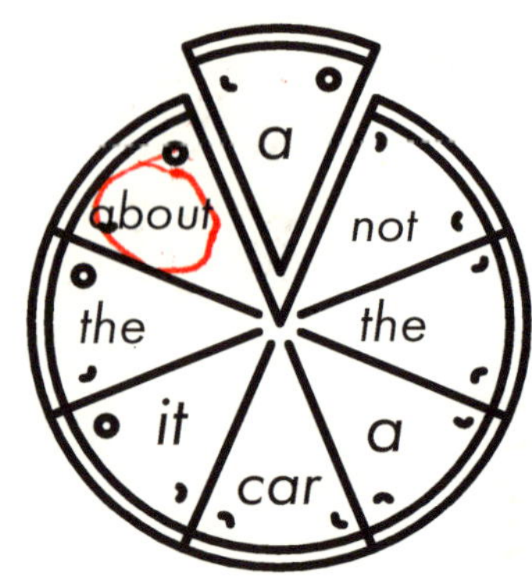

Let's work on our cutting and pasting skills. Cut out the letter "**about**" from page 173 and paste it in the square box below to complete the sentence. Then read the sentence aloud!

What is this story about?

Write your own sentence using the word **about**:

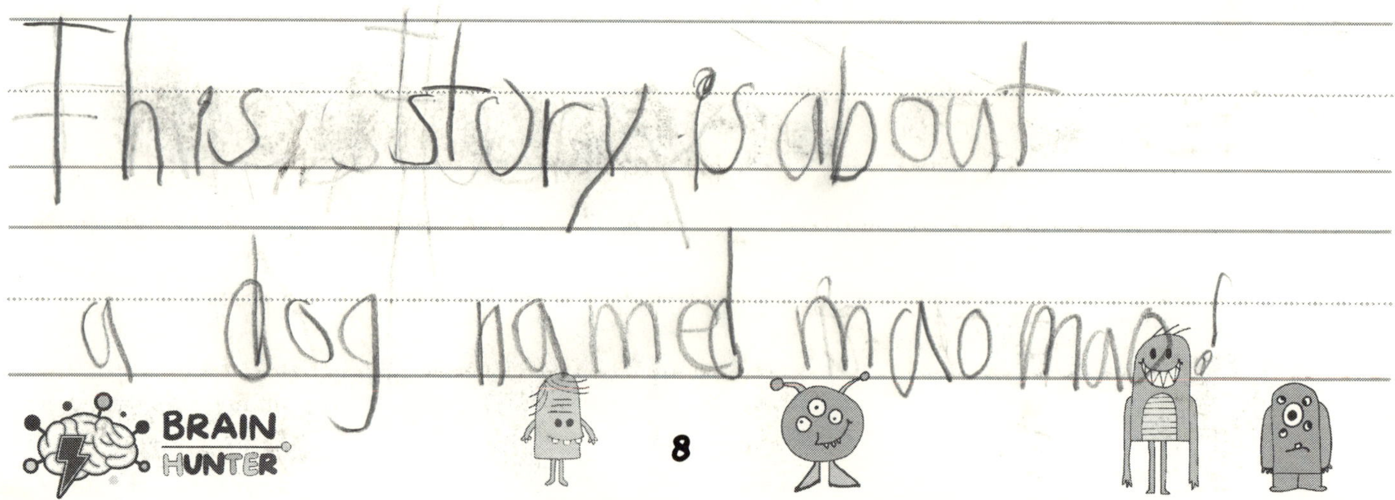

BRAIN HUNTER

My uncle lives **above** me.

Trace the word:

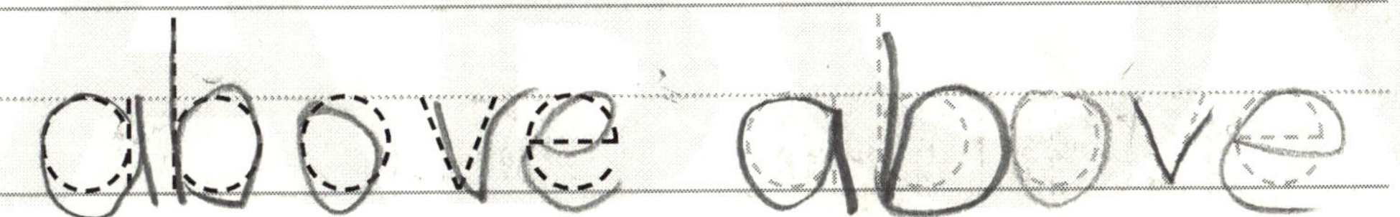

Write the word:

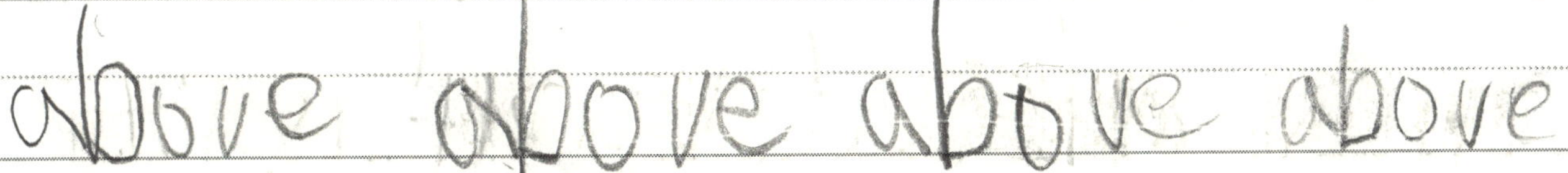

Color the puzzle pieces that have the word "**above**"

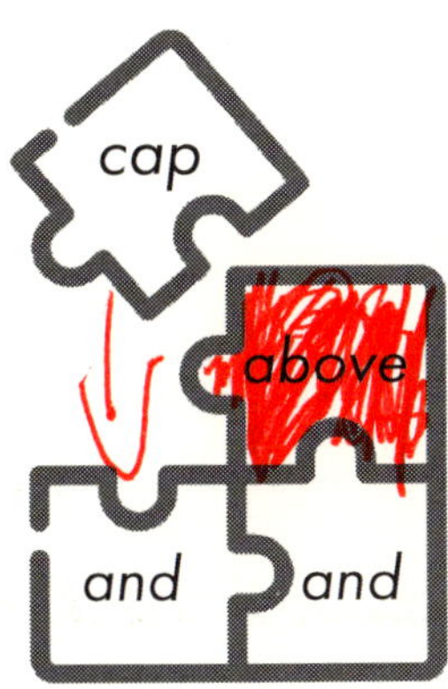

Find and circle the word "**above**"

Fill in the missing letters to make the word "**above**"

a _ _ ve **_ _ ove**

_ _ _ ve **a _ _ v _**

_ _ _ v _ **_ _ _ _ _**

My uncle lives _ _ _ _ _ me.

Write your own sentence using the word **above**:

BRAIN HUNTER

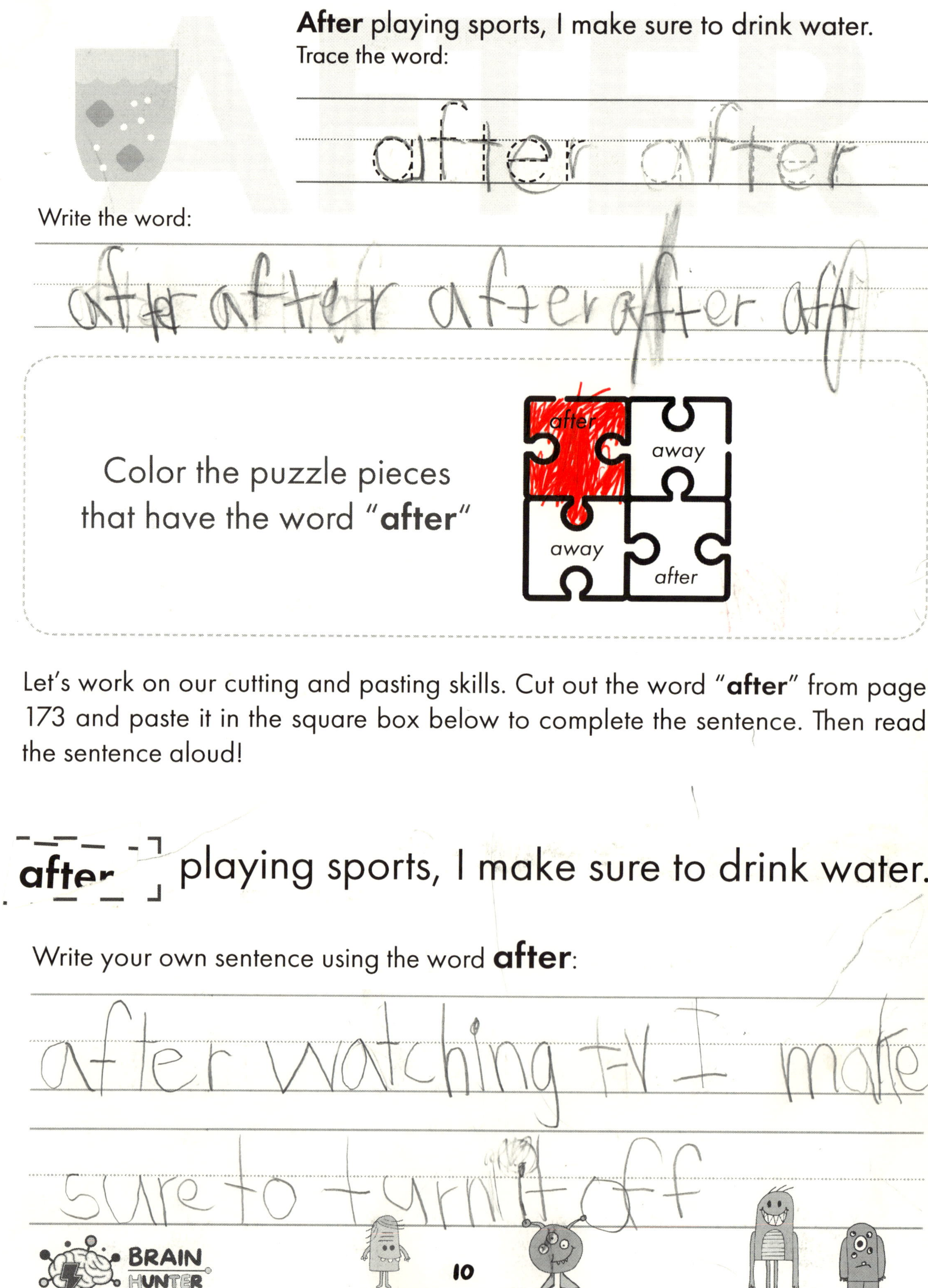

After playing sports, I make sure to drink water.

Trace the word:

after after

Write the word:

Color the puzzle pieces that have the word "**after**"

Let's work on our cutting and pasting skills. Cut out the word "**after**" from page 173 and paste it in the square box below to complete the sentence. Then read the sentence aloud!

after playing sports, I make sure to drink water.

Write your own sentence using the word **after**:

It's raining **again**!

Trace the word:

again again

Write the word:

Color the pizza slices that have the word "**again**"

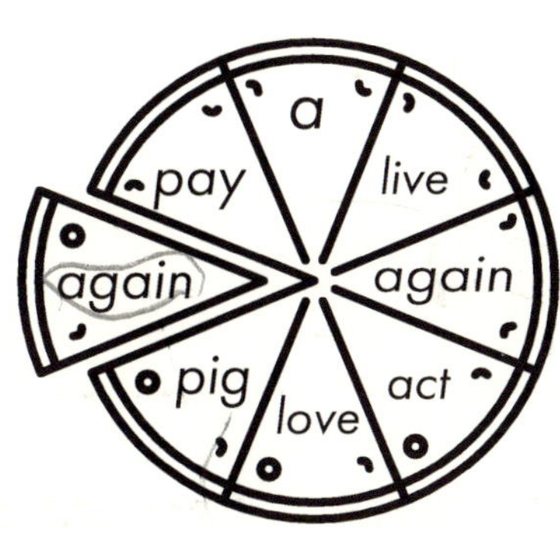

Find and circle the word "**again**"

Fill in the missing letters to make the word "**again**"

ag__n **aga__**

_g_i_ **___in**

____n **a__i_**

Write your own sentence using the word **again**:

We are **almost** there.

Trace the word:

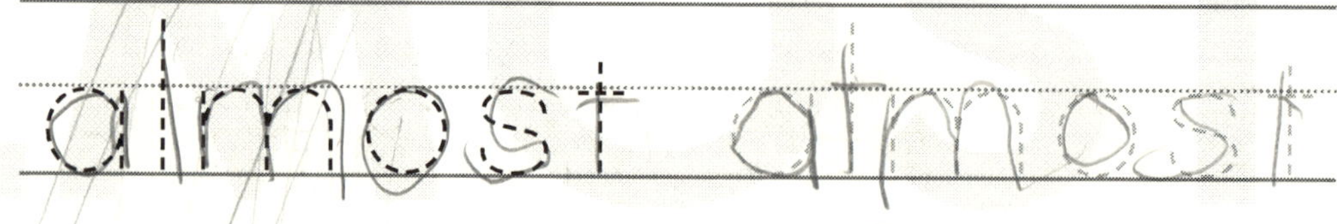

Write the word:

Color the star that has the word "**almost**"

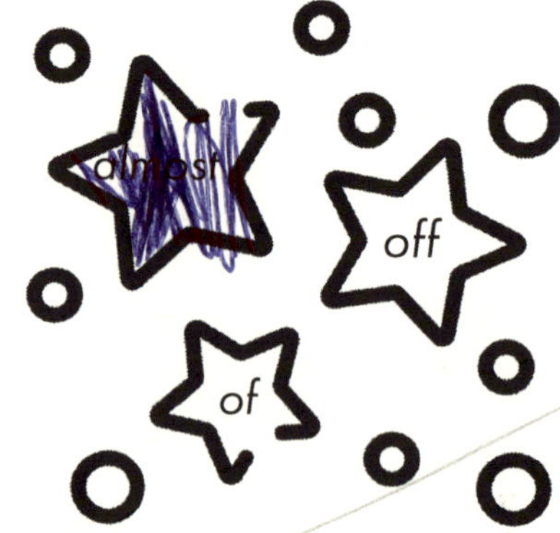

Let's work on our cutting and pasting skills. Cut out the word "**almost**" from page 173 and paste it in the square box below to complete the sentence. Then read the sentence aloud!

We are almost there.

Write your own sentence using the word **almost**:

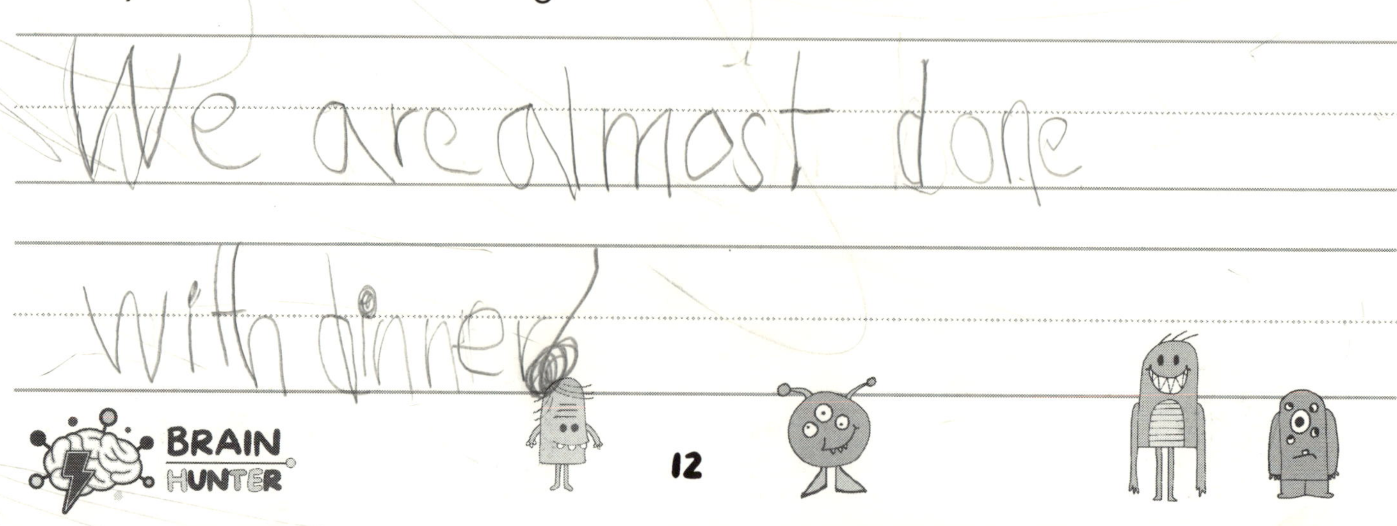

My mom is looking for **another** job.

Trace the word:

another another

Write the word:

Color the pie pieces that have the word "**another**"

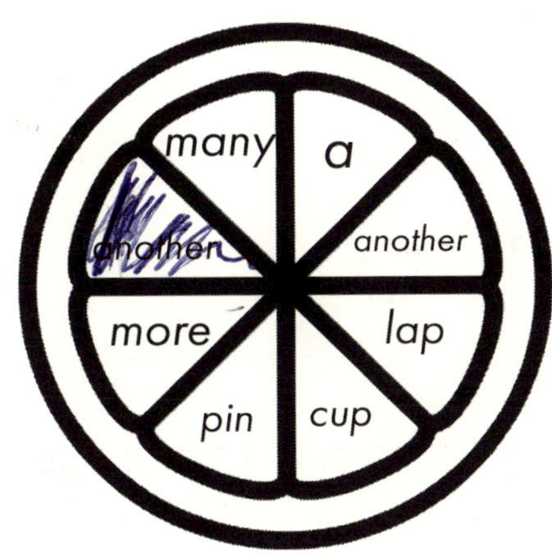

Find and circle the word "**another**"

l r u n b p a
z q e z r n z
ż k f h o l z
x e e t w e x
r s h y q q p
m e b m z m u
r o f s o z x

Fill in the missing letters to make the word "**another**"

an__her a__ther

_n_ther a_____

____r _____

My mom is looking for_ _ _ _ _ _ _ job.

Write your own sentence using the word **another**:

We **are** from Europe.

Trace the word:

Write the word:

Color the pizza slices that have the word "**are**"

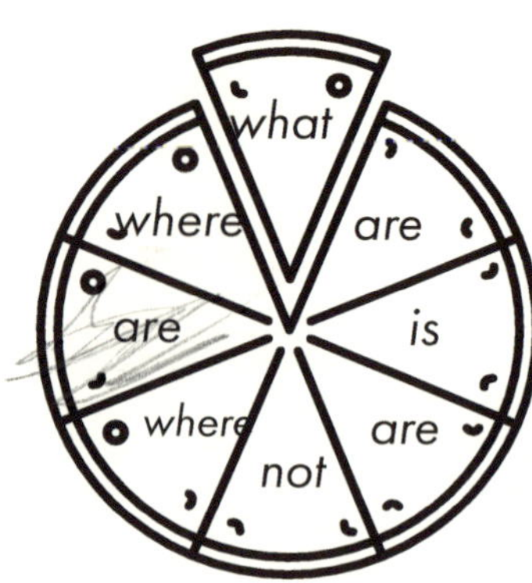

Let's work on our cutting and pasting skills. Cut out the word "**are**" from page 173 and paste it in the square box below to complete the sentence. Then read the sentence aloud!

We are from Europe.

Write your own sentence using the word **are**:

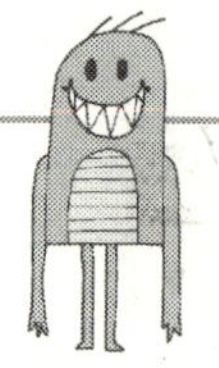

Kim wants to travel **around** the world.

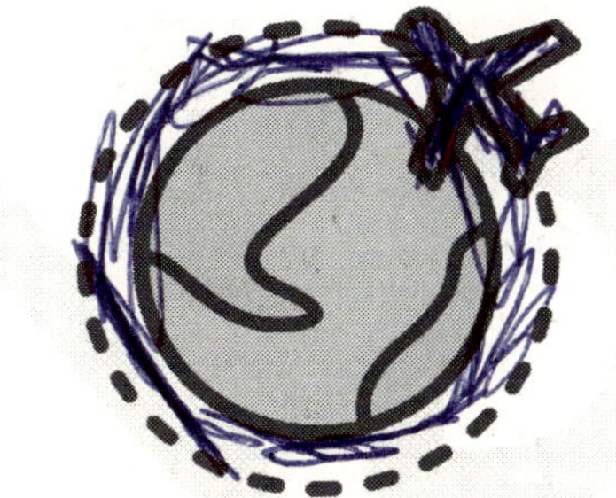

Trace the word:

around around

Write the word:

Color the puzzle pieces that have the word "**around**"

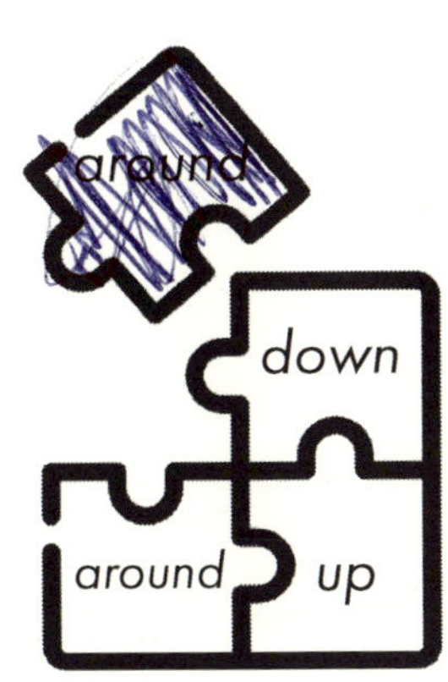

Find and circle the word "**around**"

y	q	j	z	z	a	d
d	d	t	t	x	r	z
r	r	p	b	g	o	w
j	z	h	o	x	u	m
k	n	j	l	u	n	t
y	g	e	n	e	d	g
f	m	j	t	w	f	c

Fill in the missing letters to make the word "**around**"

aro__d **___und**

a_o_n_ **__ou__**

a___nd **______**

Kim wants to travel ______ the world.

Write your own sentence using the word **around**:

BRAIN HUNTER

Roses are **beautiful.**

Trace the word:

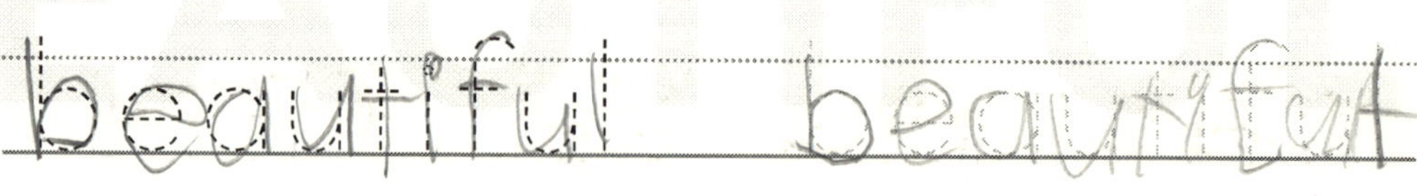

Write the word:

Color the puzzle pieces that have the word "**beautiful**"

Let's work on our cutting and pasting skills. Cut out the word "**beautiful**" from page 173 and paste it in the square box below to complete the sentence. Then read the sentence aloud!

Write your own sentence using the word **beautiful**:

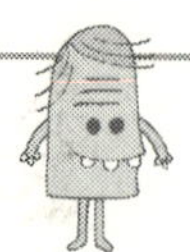

I am a good student **because** I study.

Trace the word:

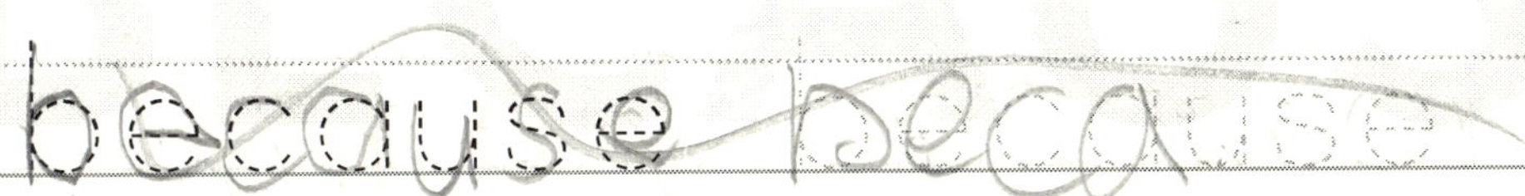

Write the word:

Color the pizza slices that have the word "**because**"

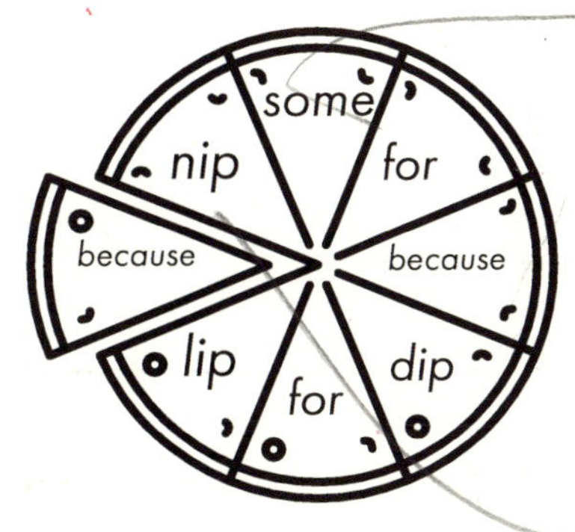

Find and circle the word "**because**"

l	m	a	b	c	w	g
w	s	e	d	t	l	y
e	b	q	g	t	a	w
m	q	a	i	b	i	z
n	n	z	c	d	x	h
e	s	u	a	c	e	b
v	e	j	u	b	h	t

Fill in the missing letters to make the word "**because**"

be_____ b__ause

___ause _____se

______e _______

_ _ _ _ _ _ _ **I study**

Write your own sentence using the word **because**:

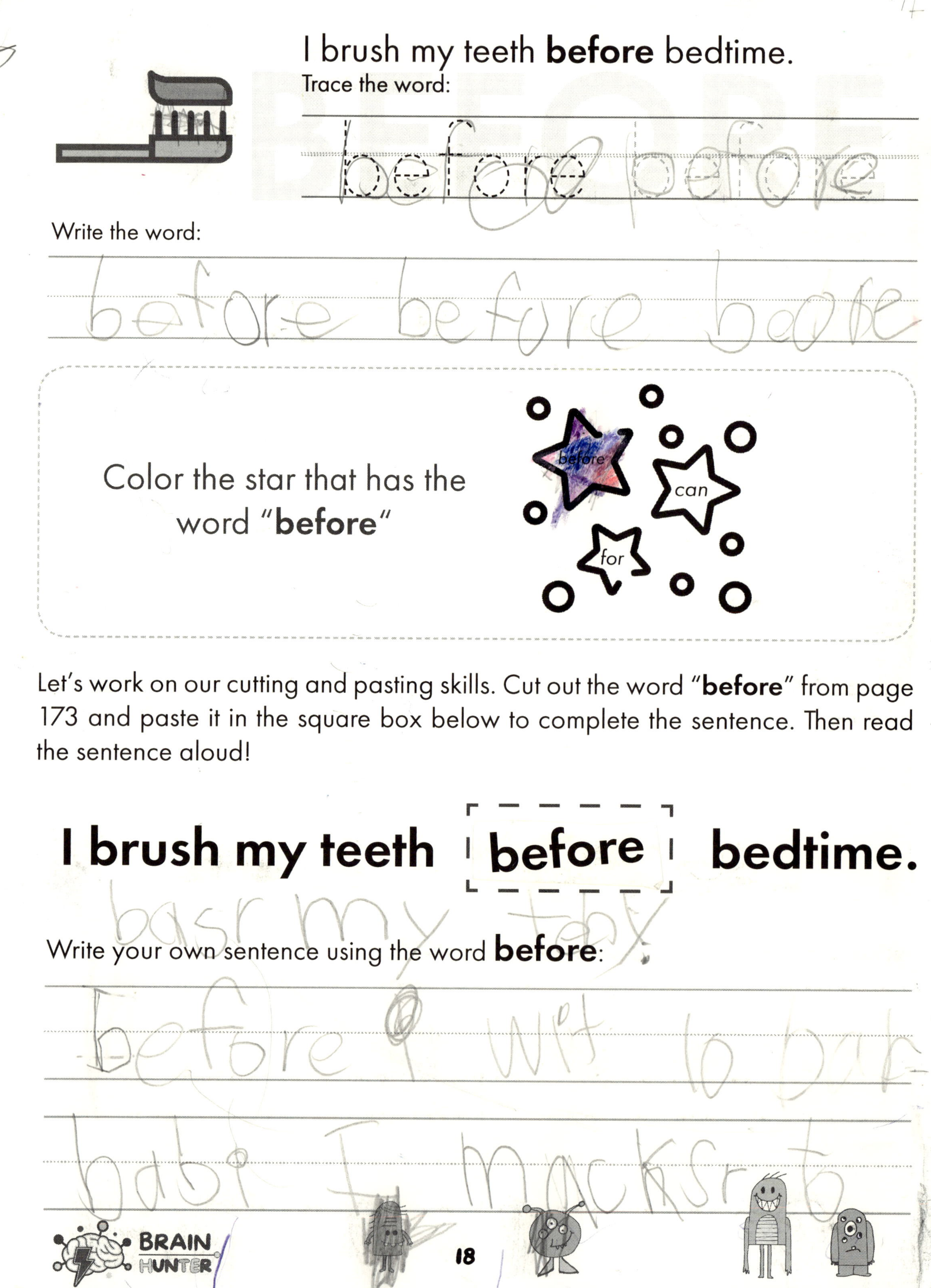

I brush my teeth **before** bedtime.

Trace the word:

before

Write the word:

Color the star that has the word "**before**"

Let's work on our cutting and pasting skills. Cut out the word "**before**" from page 173 and paste it in the square box below to complete the sentence. Then read the sentence aloud!

I brush my teeth before bedtime.

Write your own sentence using the word **before**:

I don't like **being** late.

Trace the word:

Write the word:

Color the pie pieces that have the word "**being**"

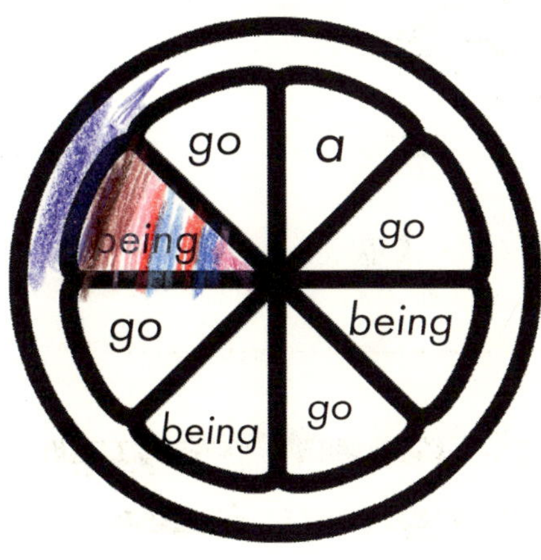

Find and circle the word "**being**"

s	r	d	s	b
b	e	i	n	g
f	z	a	x	n
s	g	k	b	i
p	u	u	t	v

Fill in the missing letters to make the word "**being**"

__ __ **ing** **b** __ **ing**

__ __ __ **ng** __ **e** __ **n** __

__ __ **i** __ __ __ __ __ __ __

I don't like __ __ __ __ __ late.

Write your own sentence using the word **being**:

Mary is the **best** student in the class.

Trace the word:

Write the word:

Color the pizza slices that have the word "**best**"

Let's work on our cutting and pasting skills. Cut out the word "**best**" from page 173 and paste it in the square box below to complete the sentence. Then read the sentence aloud!

Mary is the [ ] student.

Write your own sentence using the word **best**:

She is wearing **black** socks.

Trace the word:

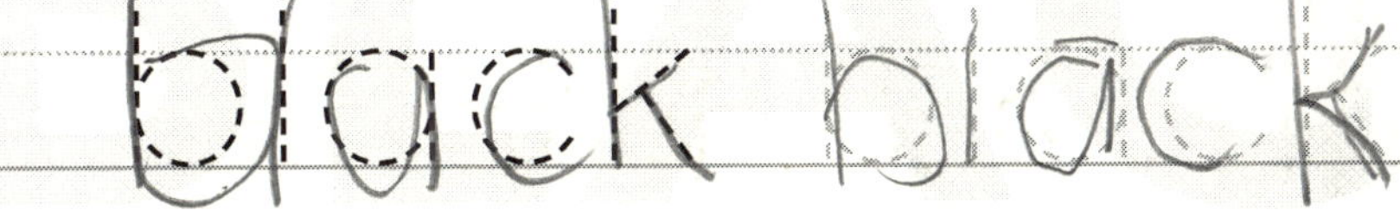

Write the word:

Color the puzzle pieces that have the word "**black**"

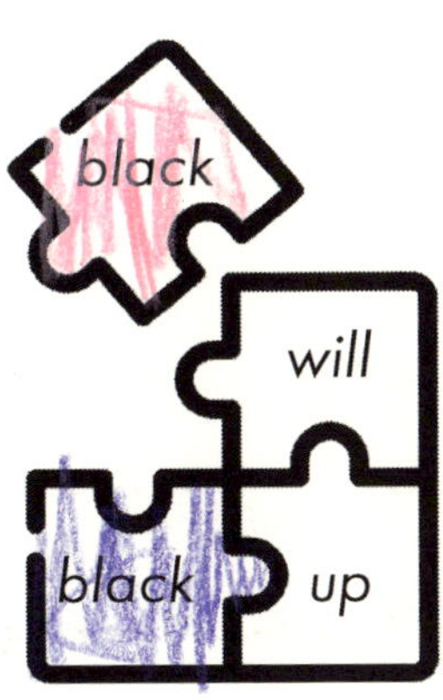

Find and circle the word "**black**"

Fill in the missing letters to make the word "**black**"

bl_ _k **b_ _ck**

b_ _ _k **_ _ _c_**

_ _ac_ **_ _ _ _ _**

She is wearing _ _ _ _ _ socks.

Write your own sentence using the word **black**:

I have three **brothers** and one sister.

Trace the word:

brothers brothers

Write the word:

Color the puzzle pieces that have the word "**brothers**"

Let's work on our cutting and pasting skills. Cut out the word "**brothers**" from page 173 and paste it in the square box below to complete the sentence. Then read the sentence aloud!

Three brothers and one sister.

Write your own sentence using the word **brothers**:

My friend is afraid of **bugs.**

Trace the word:

bugs bugs bugs

Write the word:

Color the pizza slices that have the word "**bugs**"

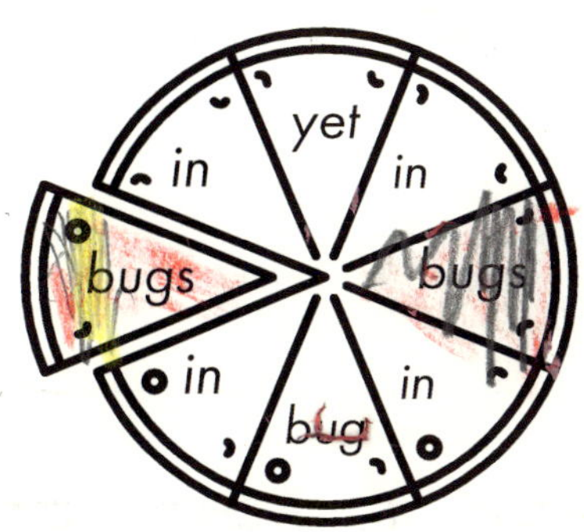

Find and circle the word "**bugs**"

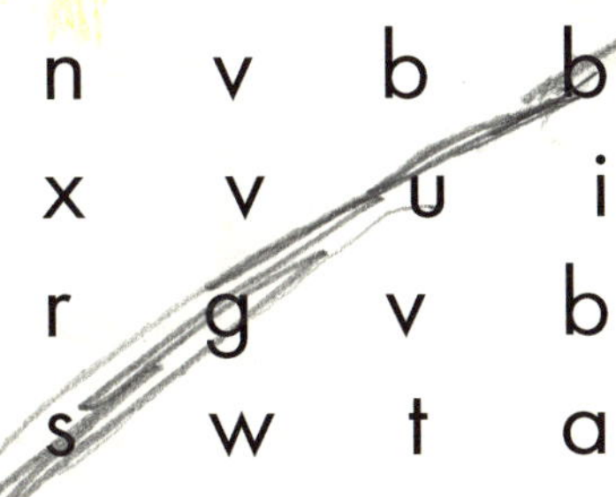

n	v	b	b
x	v	u	i
r	g	v	b
s	w	t	a

Fill in the missing letters to make the word "**bugs**"

bu_s   __gs

___s   b_g_

b__s   ____

My friend is afraid of _ _ _ _

Write your own sentence using the word **bugs**:

Mike's shirt is **blue.**

Trace the word:

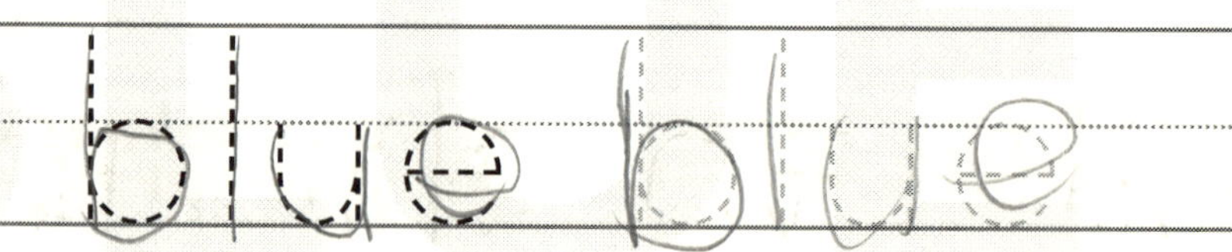

Write the word:

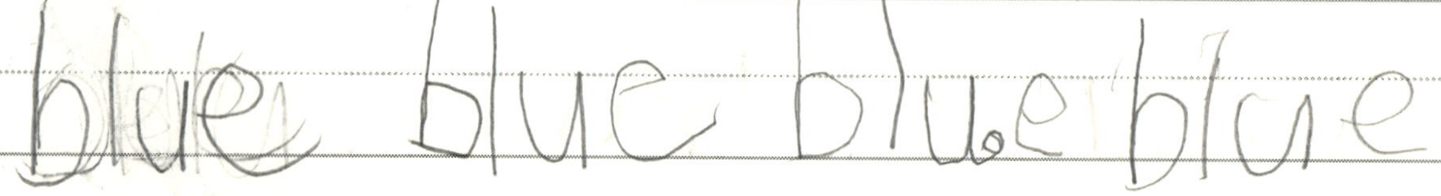

Color the star that has the word "**blue**"

Let's work on our cutting and pasting skills. Cut out the word "**blue**" from page 173 and paste it in the square box below to complete the sentence. Then read the sentence aloud!

Mike's shirt is  .

Write your own sentence using the word **blue**:

There are twelve **children** in the class.

Trace the word:

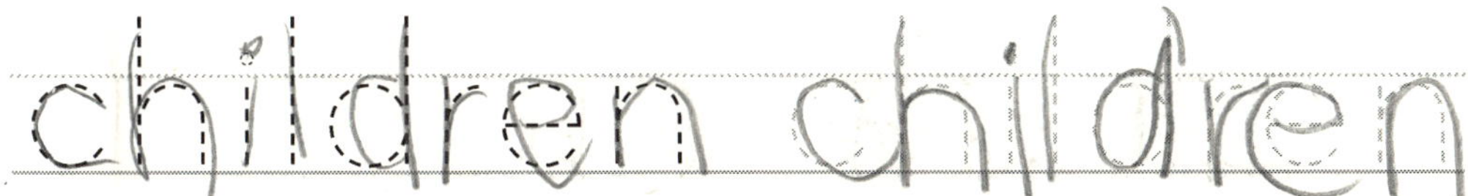

Write the word:

Color the pie pieces that have the word "**children**"

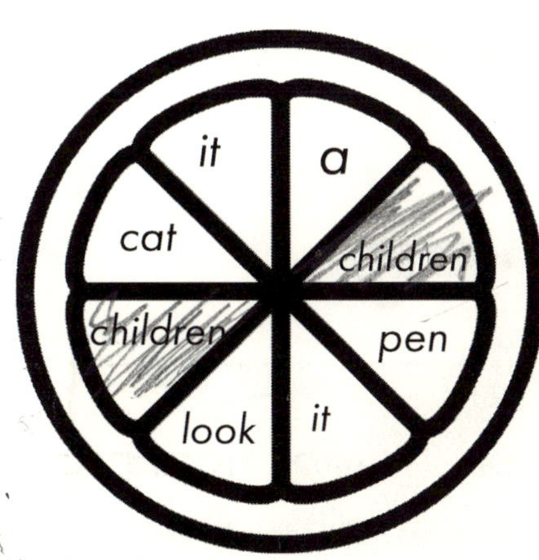

Find and circle the word "**children**"

Fill in the missing letters to make the word "**children**"

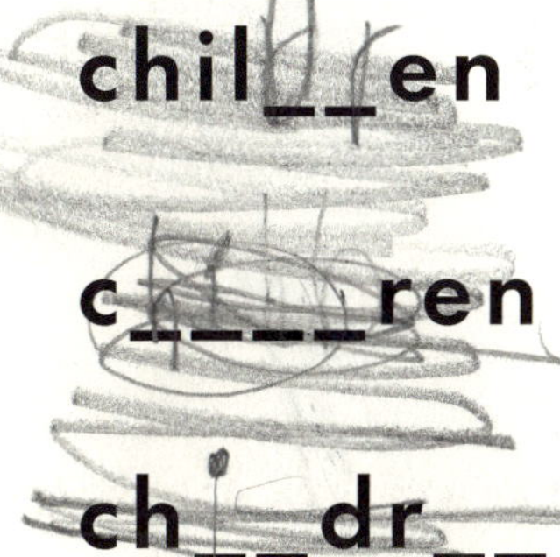

There are twelve _ _ _ _ _ _ _ _ in the class.

Write your own sentence using the word **children**:

The **clock** stopped working.

Trace the word:

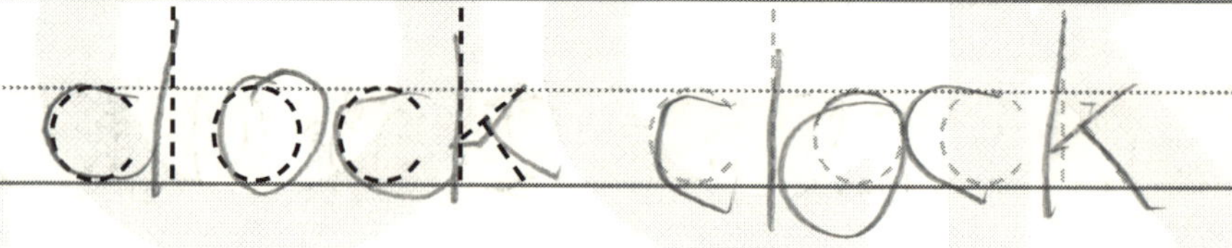

Write the word:

Color the pizza slices that have the word "**clock**"

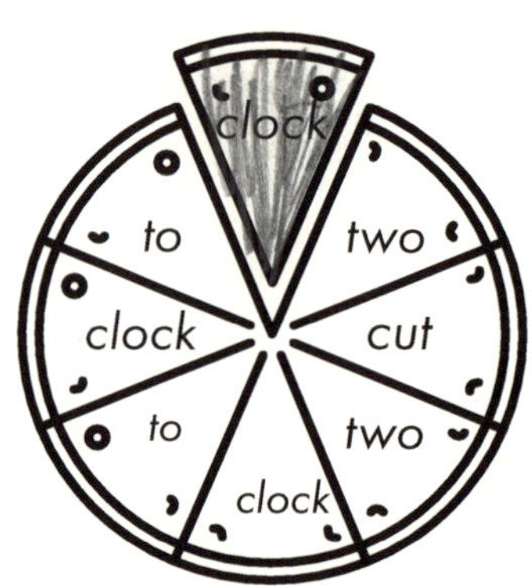

Let's work on our cutting and pasting skills. Cut out the word "**clock**" from page 173 and paste it in the square box below to complete the sentence. Then read the sentence aloud!

The [ ] stopped working.

Write your own sentence using the word **clock**:

Do you know the seven **colors** in a rainbow?

Trace the word:

colors colors

Write the word:

Color the puzzle pieces that have the word "**colors**"

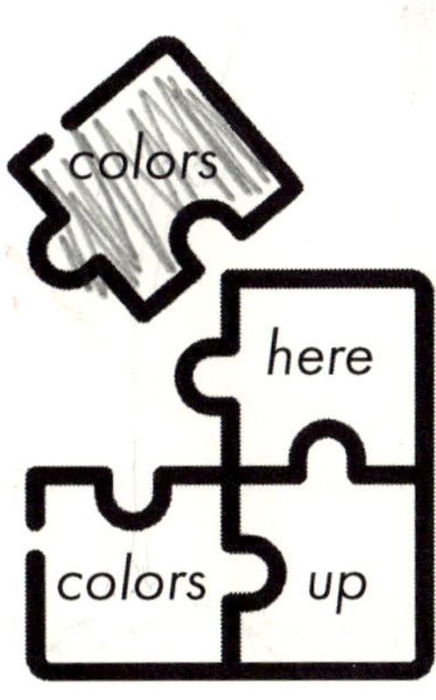

Find and circle the word "**colors**"

n	d	s	z	p	y
e	n	r	k	l	b
w	q	o	b	j	o
v	b	l	y	p	z
f	v	o	w	k	l
b	w	c	u	k	b

Fill in the missing letters to make the word "**colors**"

col_ _ co_o_ _

_ _l_ _s _o_o_s

_ _ _o_ _ _ _ _ _ _ _

There are seven _ _ _ _ _ _ in a rainbow.

Write your own sentence using the word **colors**:

Could I use your desk?

Trace the word:

Write the word:

Color the puzzle pieces that have the word "**could**"

Let's work on our cutting and pasting skills. Cut out the word "**could**" from page 173 and paste it in the square box below to complete the sentence. Then read the sentence aloud!

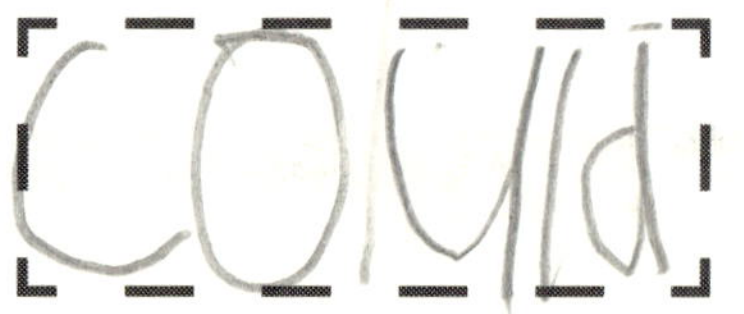 **I use your desk?**

Write your own sentence using the word **could**:

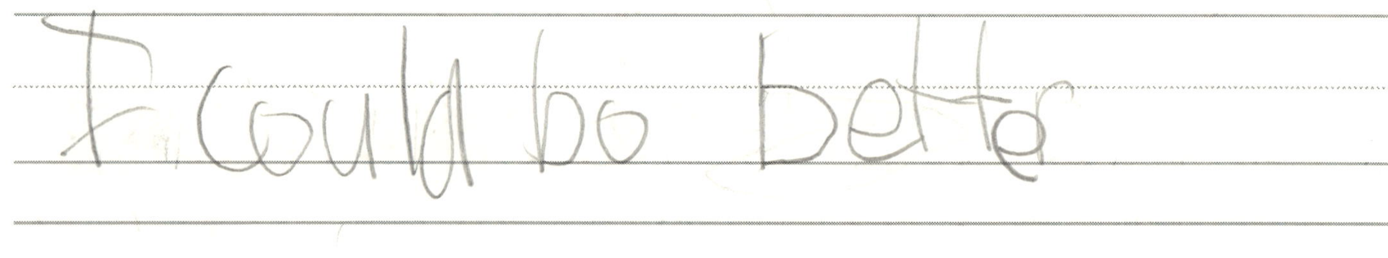

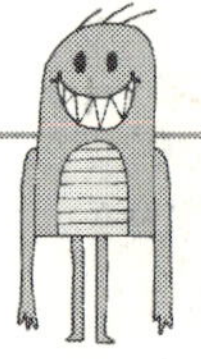

Didn't you come to the party yesterday?

Trace the word:

didn't didn't

Write the word:

Color the pizza slices that have the word "**didn't**"

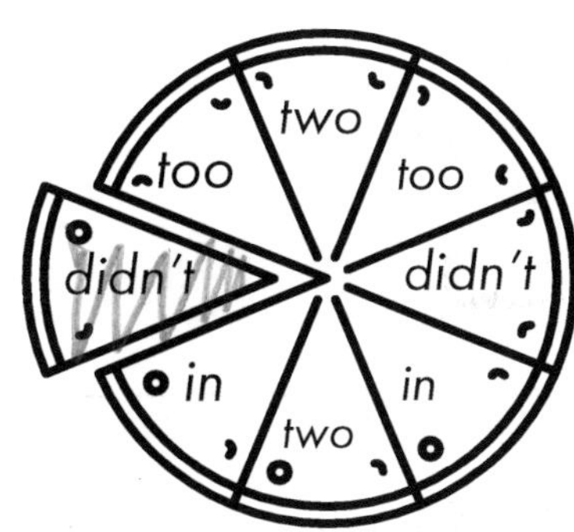

Find and circle the word "**didn't**"

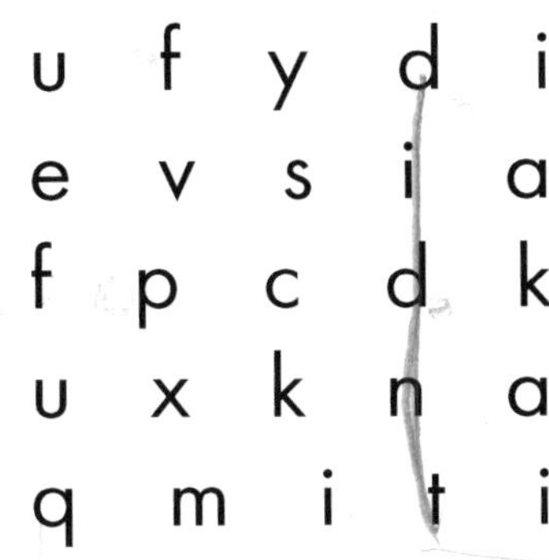

Fill in the missing letters to make the word "**didn't**"

di__'t did_'t

__dn't ____'t

____'t ____'t

____'_ **you come to the party yesterday?**

Write your own sentence using the word **didn't**:

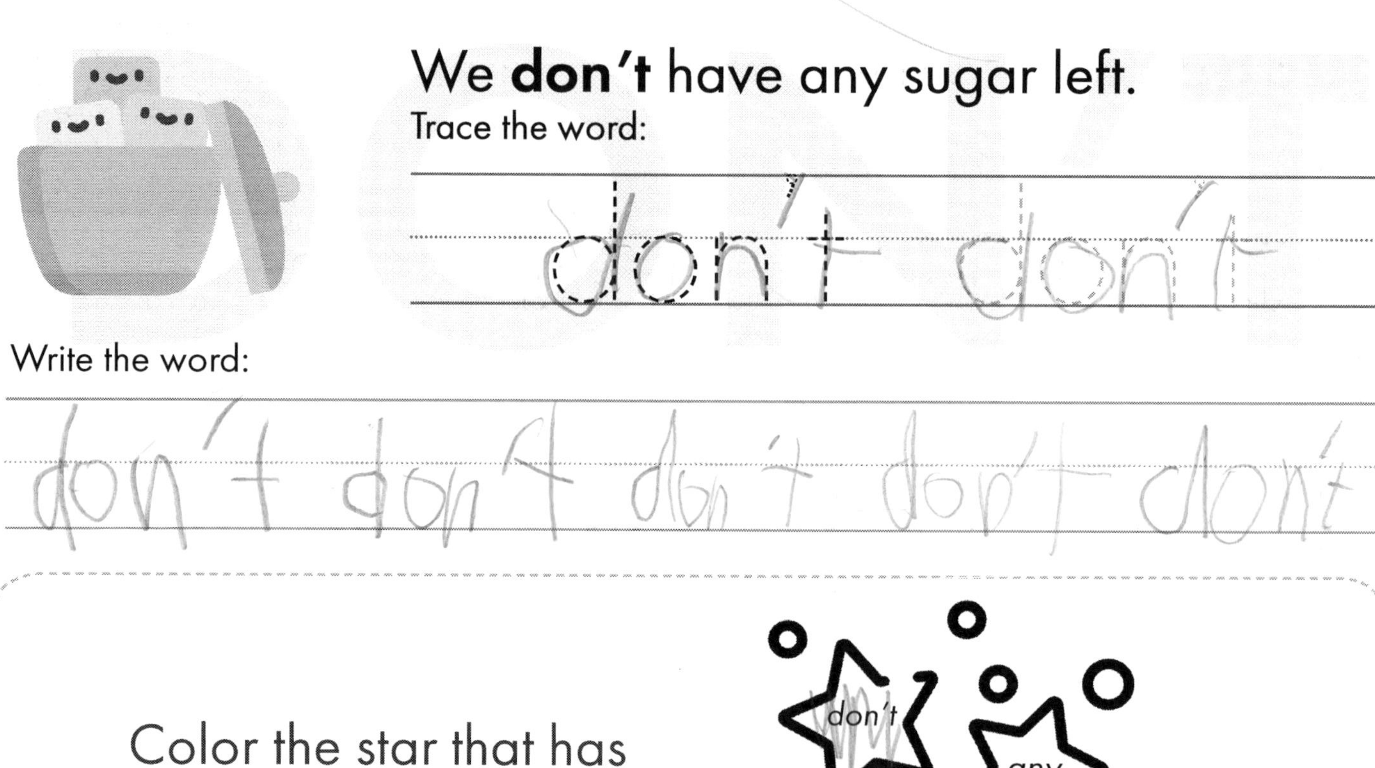

We **don't** have any sugar left.

Trace the word:

Write the word:

Color the star that has the word "**don't**"

Let's work on our cutting and pasting skills. Cut out the word "**don't**" from page 173 and paste it in the square box below to complete the sentence. Then read the sentence aloud!

We [ ] have any sugar left.

Write your own sentence using the word **don't**:

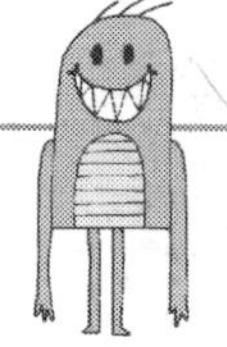

I am almost **done** with my homework.

Trace the word:

done done done

Write the word:

Color the pie pieces that have the word "**done**"

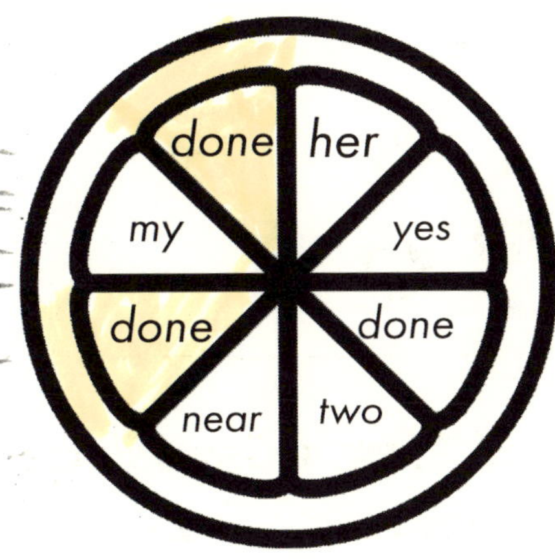

Find and circle the word "**done**"

u	e	g	h
f	n	d	j
r	o	e	z
r	d	p	i

Fill in the missing letters to make the word "**done**"

don_ do_e

_o_e d__e

___e ____

I am almost ____ with my homework .

Write your own sentence using the word **done**:

Does Julia play the piano?

Trace the word:

Write the word:

Color the pizza slices that have the word "**does**"

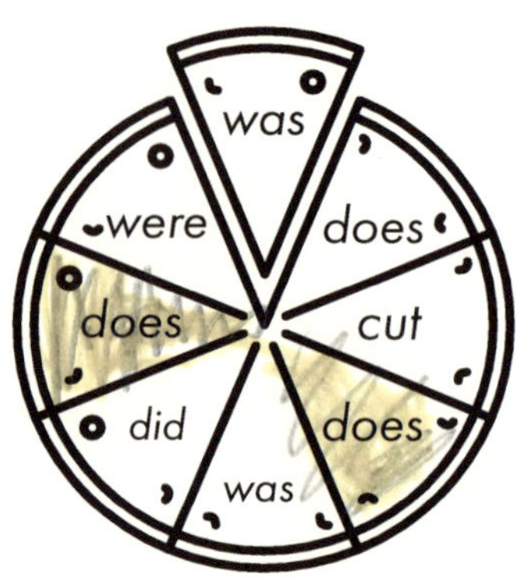

Let's work on our cutting and pasting skills. Cut out the word "**does**" from page 173 and paste it in the square box below to complete the sentence. Then read the sentence aloud!

 **Julia play the piano?**

Write your own sentence using the word **does**:

They admire **each** other.

Trace the word:

Write the word:

Color the puzzle pieces that have the word "**each**"

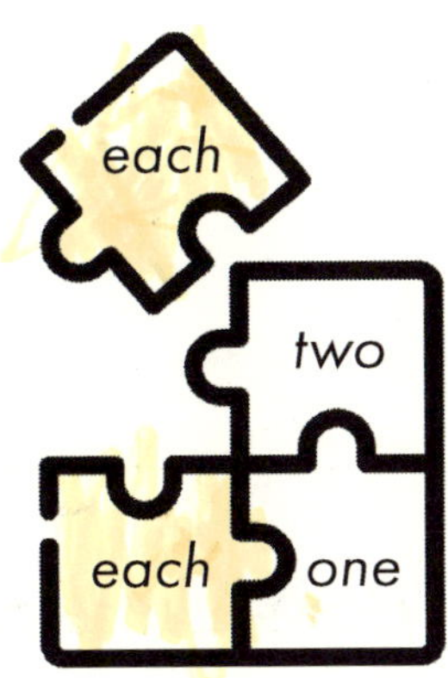

Find and circle the word "**each**"

v	e	h	s	j	y
v	x	n	c	p	w
c	j	v	a	a	n
o	v	i	s	y	e
h	v	d	j	j	o
c	c	p	y	c	y

Fill in the missing letters to make the word "**each**"

ea_h **ea__**

_a_h **__c_**

e__h **____**

They admire ____ other.

Write your own sentence using the word **each**:

BRAIN HUNTER

A stop sign has **eight** sides.

Trace the word:

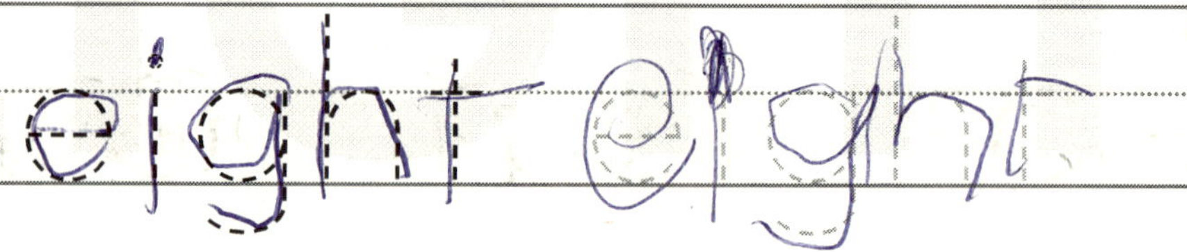

Write the word:

Color the puzzle pieces that have the word "**eight**"

Let's work on our cutting and pasting skills. Cut out the word "**eight**" from page 173 and paste it in the square box below to complete the sentence. Then read the sentence aloud!

A stop sign has [ ] sides.

Write your own sentence using the word **eight**:

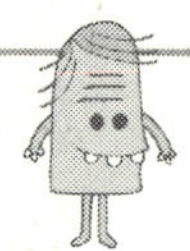

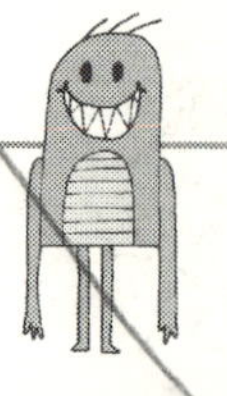

I like to **eat** apples.

Trace the word:

Write the word:

Color the pizza slices that have the word "**eat**"

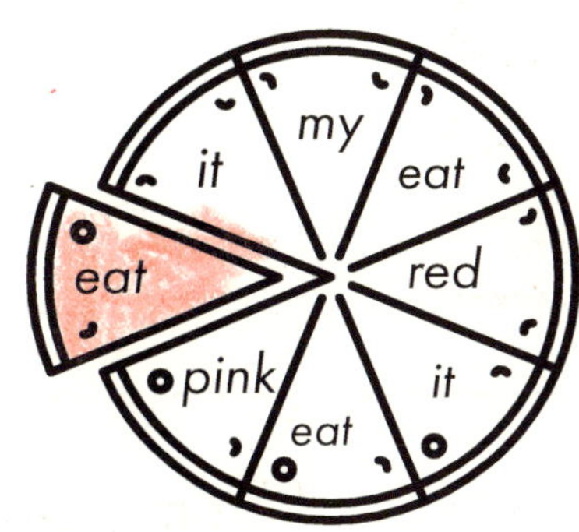

Find and circle the word "**eat**"

o s f i n d
m k f w y w
k b p u k x
o l d e d y
k e a e l i
k t w p l m

Fill in the missing letters to make the word "**eat**"

_at **e_t**
e_t **ea_**
e_t **___**

I like to ___ apples.

Write your own sentence using the word **eat**:

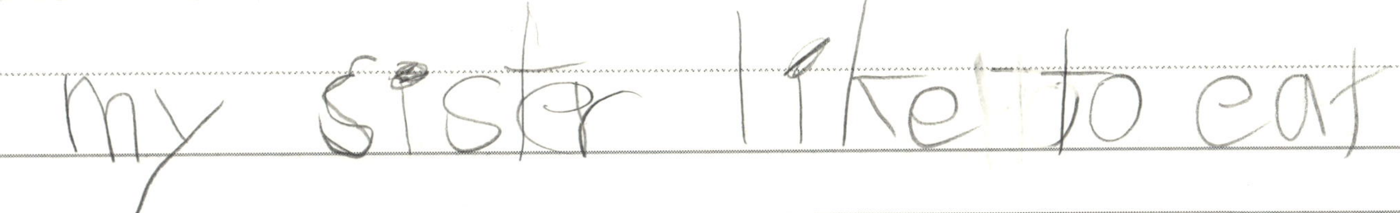

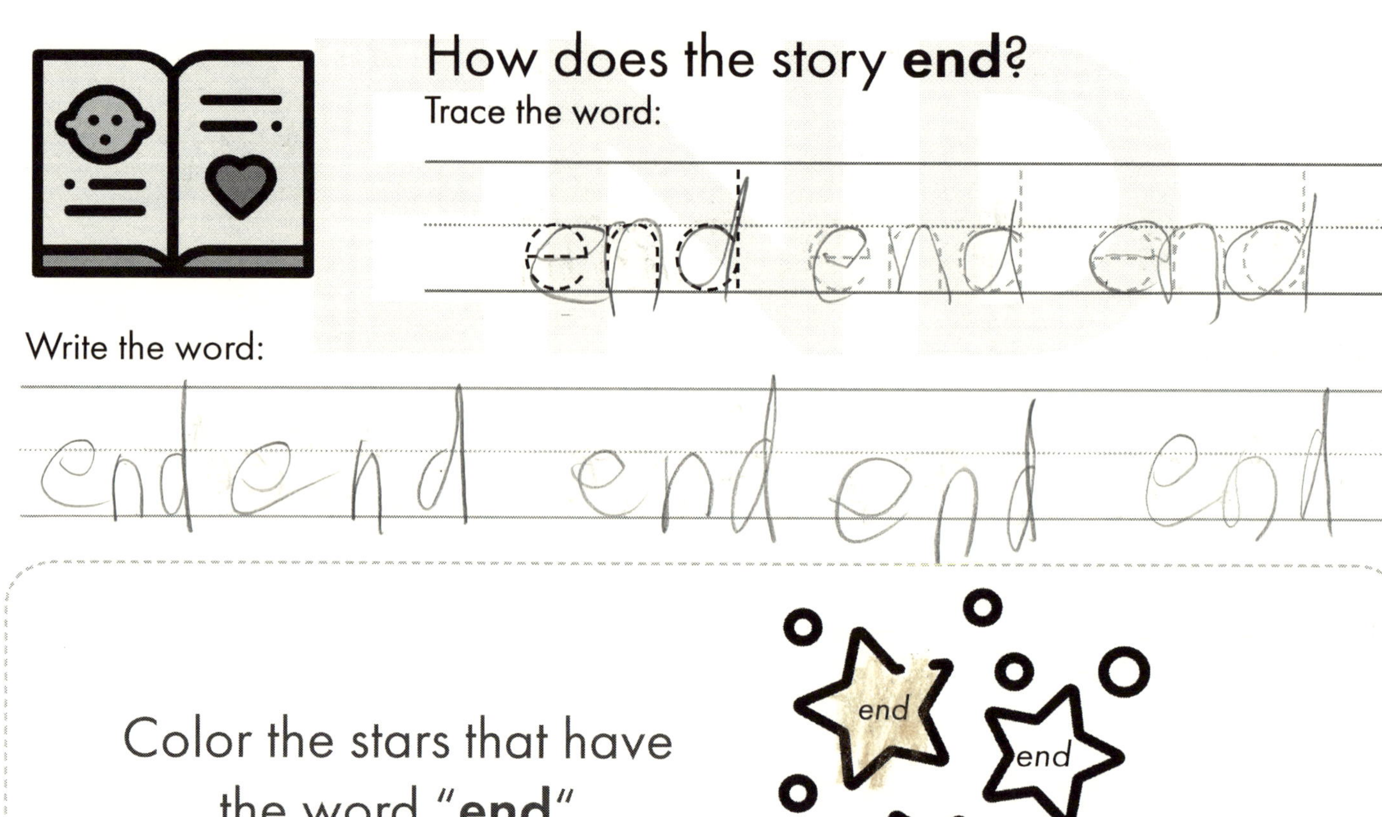

How does the story **end**?

Trace the word:

Write the word:

Color the stars that have the word "**end**"

end

end

to

Let's work on our cutting and pasting skills. Cut out the word "**end**" from page 173 and paste it in the square box below to complete the sentence. Then read the sentence aloud!

How does the story ☐?

Write your own sentence using the word **end**:

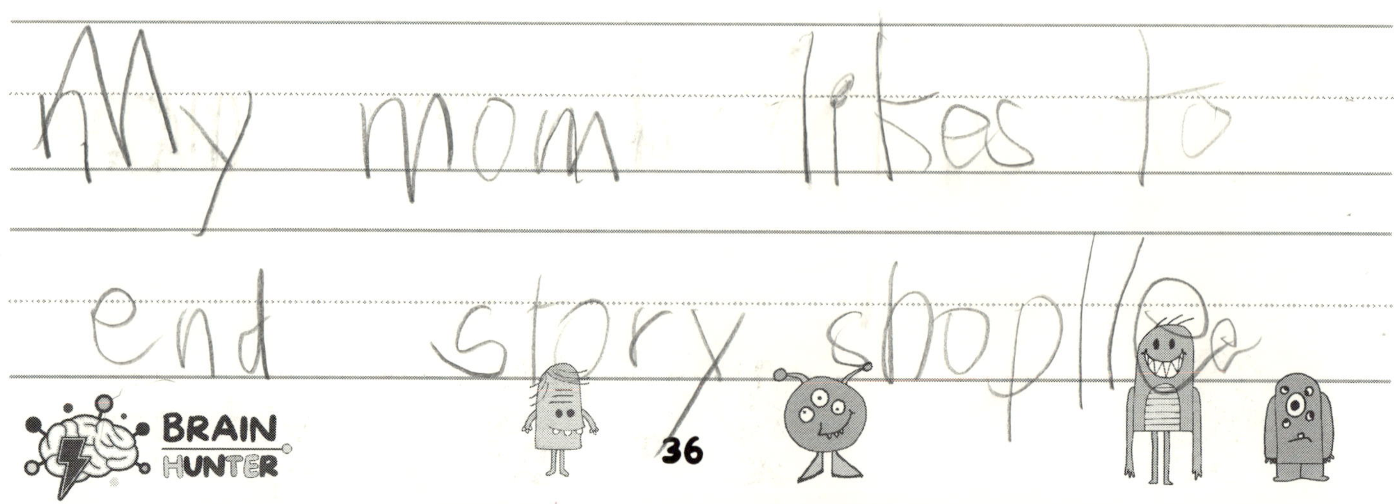

Where can I **find** toothpaste?

Trace the word:

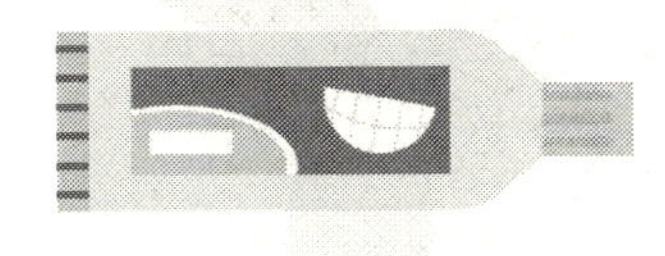

Write the word:

Color the pie pieces that have the word "**find**"

Find and circle the word "**find**"

q	d	f	g	n	d
d	n	i	f	r	x
u	u	n	x	d	v
i	d	a	u	y	a
d	g	c	z	j	o
n	a	t	i	u	p

Fill in the missing letters to make the word "**find**"

ind fi _

_ _nd f_n_

_i_d _ _ _ _

Where can I _ _ _ _ toothpaste?

Write your own sentence using the word **find**:

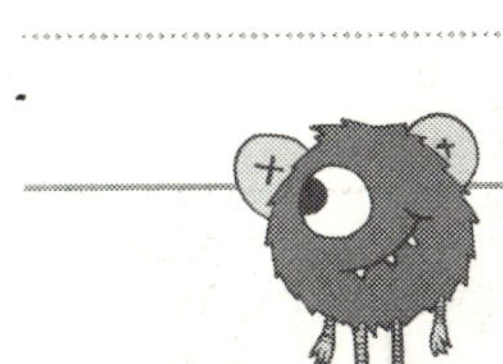

This is my first time in Japan.

Trace the word:

Write the word:

Color the pizza slices that have the word "**first**"

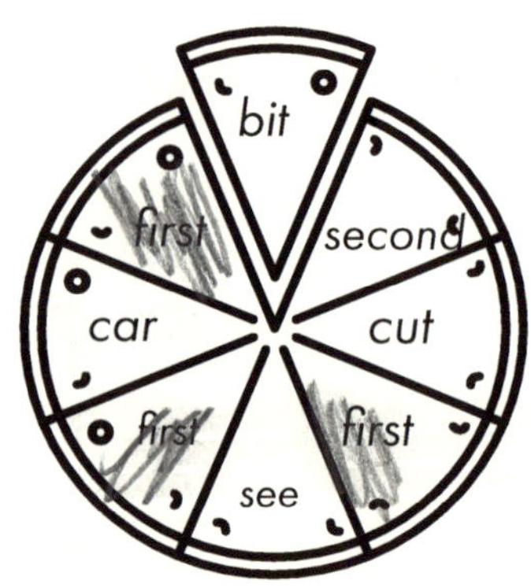

Let's work on our cutting and pasting skills. Cut out the word "**first**" from page 173 and paste it in the square box below to complete the sentence. Then read the sentence aloud!

This is my [ ] time in Japan.

Write your own sentence using the word **first**:

The traffic light is **green**.

Trace the word:

green

Write the word:

Color the puzzle pieces that have the word "**green**"

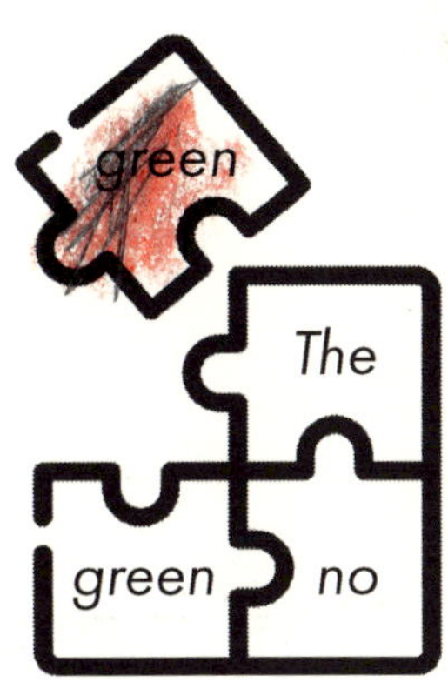

Find and circle the word "**green**"

m n z z o e
v e y l n z
g e f f z z
c r r q f c
v g w u y q
p j e p f k

Fill in the missing letters to make the word "**green**"

_ _een **g_e_n**
_ _ _en **_r_e_**
_ _ _ _ _ **gree_**

The traffic light is _ _ _ _ _.

Write your own sentence using the word **green**:

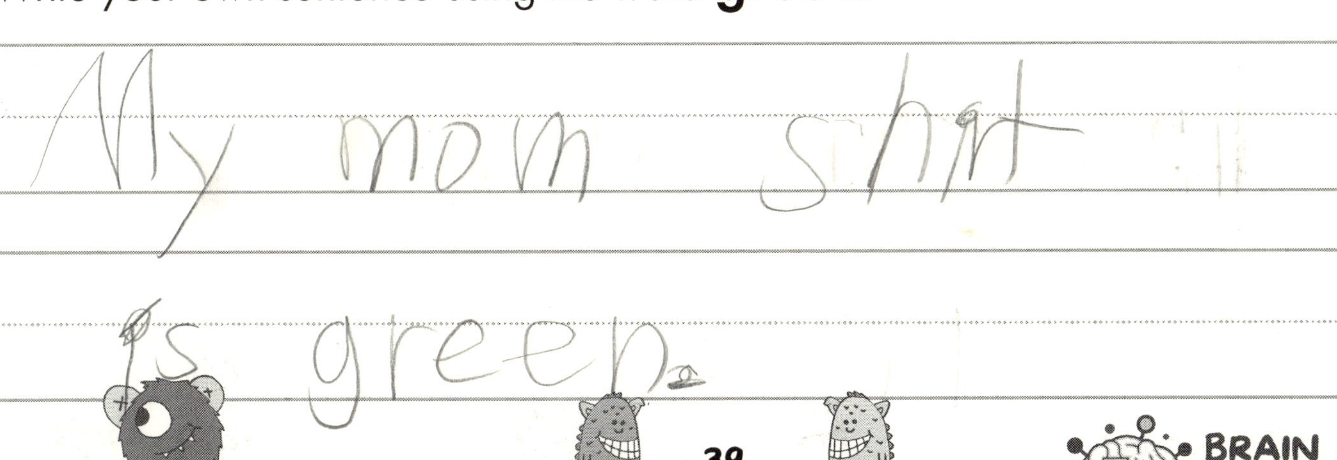

BRAIN HUNTER

Jill is a very **hard** worker.

Trace the word:

Write the word:

Color the puzzle pieces that have the word "**hard**"

hard
hard
hard
easy

Let's work on our cutting and pasting skills. Cut out the word "**hard**" from page 173 and paste it in the square box below to complete the sentence. Then read the sentence aloud!

Jill is a very [ ] worker.

Write your own sentence using the word **hard**:

Did you **hear** that?

Trace the word:

hear hear

Write the word:

Color the pizza slices that have the word "**hear**"

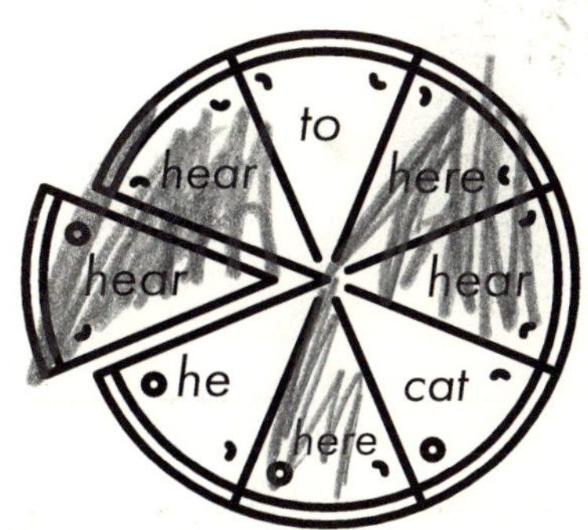

Find and circle the word "**hear**"

r	r	x	n	s	x
d	m	a	x	z	b
n	t	b	e	h	m
a	b	g	z	h	o
s	t	l	l	b	s
w	o	a	j	j	z

Fill in the missing letters to make the word "**hear**"

__ar he__

h_a_ ___r

__ar ____

Did you ____ that?.

Write your own sentence using the word **hear**:

I accidently fell and **hurt** my knee.

Trace the word:

hurt hurt hurt

Write the word:

Color the stars that have the word "**hurt**"

Let's work on our cutting and pasting skills. Cut out the word "**hurt**" from page 173 and paste it in the square box below to complete the sentence. Then read the sentence aloud!

I accidently ☐ my knee.

Write your own sentence using the word **hurt**:

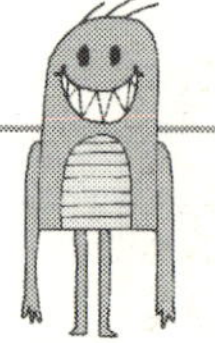

It's always sunny in Philadelphia.

Trace the word:

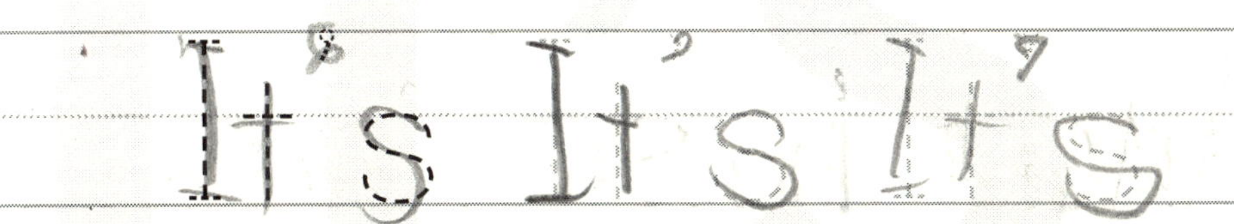

Write the word:

Color the pie pieces that have the word "**it's**"

Find and circle the word "**it's**"

z w z z p w
y h d w c p
k z e j i u
o i i l w i
z p t y p w
a u s d o j

Fill in the missing letters to make the word "**it's**"

_t's i_'s

it'_ _ _'s

i_'_ i_'_

_ _' _ **always sunny in Philadelphia.**

Write your own sentence using the word **it's**:

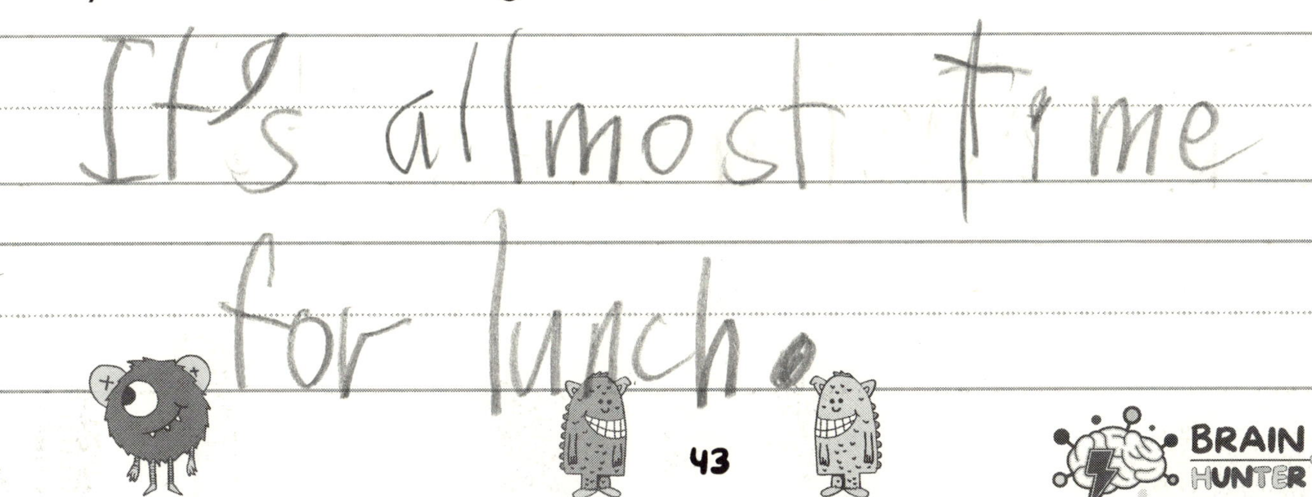

The train **just** left.

Trace the word:

just just just

Write the word:

Color the pizza slices that have the word "**just**"

We he she just just just it is

Let's work on our cutting and pasting skills. Cut out the word "**just**" from page 173 and paste it in the square box below to complete the sentence. Then read the sentence aloud!

The train [ ] left.

Write your own sentence using the word **just**:

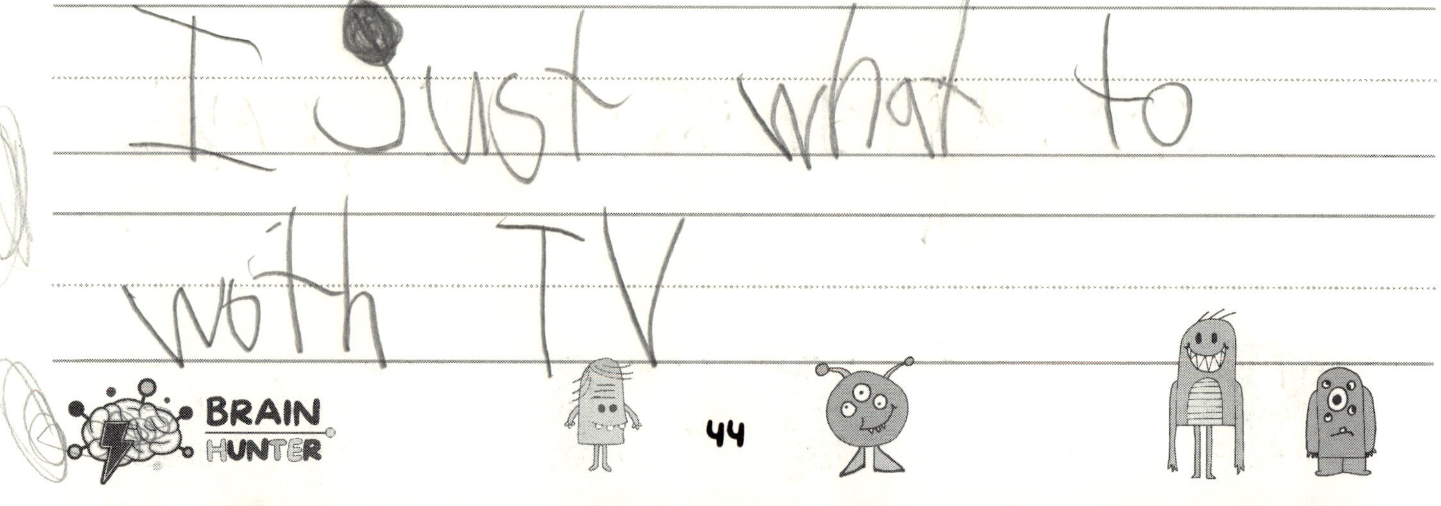

Do you **know** her name?

Trace the word:

know

Write the word:

Color the puzzle pieces that have the word "**know**"	Find and circle the word "**know**"	Fill in the missing letters to make the word "**know**"

l	w	f	v	y	k
z	f	g	t	o	n
p	s	p	l	w	o
m	d	u	i	y	w
g	x	u	j	u	j
h	f	j	l	b	m

_now   k_o_

___w   _n_w

k___   ____

Do you ____ her name?

Write your own sentence using the word **know:**

My dad works for a **large** company.

Trace the word:

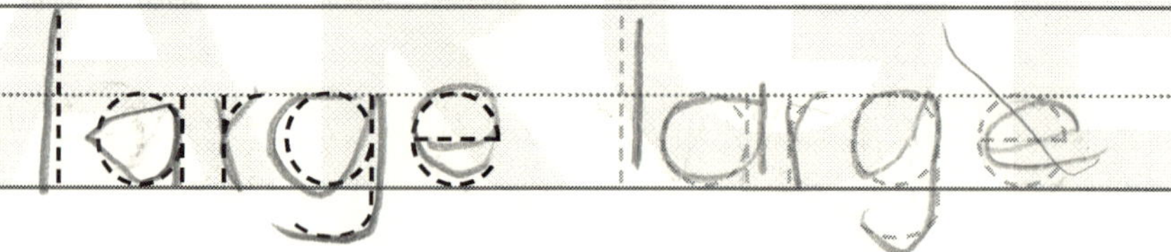

Write the word:

Color the puzzle pieces that have the word "**large**"

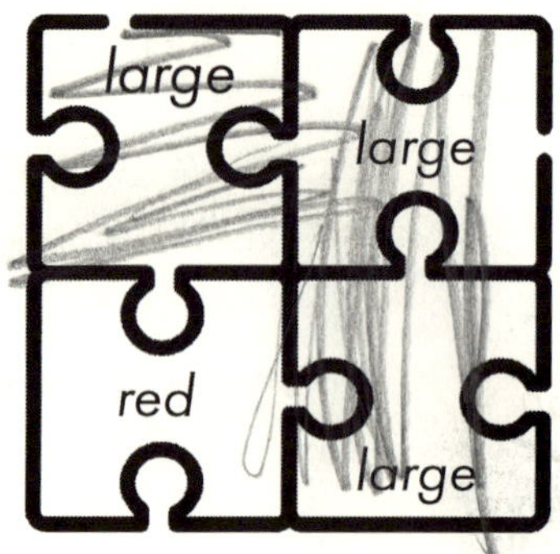

Let's work on our cutting and pasting skills. Cut out the word "**large**" from page 175 and paste it in the square box below to complete the sentence. Then read the sentence aloud!

My dad works for a ☐ company.

Write your own sentence using the word **large**:

I am **never** late to school.

Trace the word:

never never

Write the word:

Color the pizza slices that have the word "**never**"

Find and circle the word "**never**"

r f f y n g
o f w e u i
c a v c j e
i e a p y z
r h x s y z
q l d q i t

Fill in the missing letters to make the word "**never**"

___er ne_er

___r n_v_r

n____ _____

I am _____ late to school.

Write your own sentence using the word **never**:

My teacher retires **next** year.

Trace the word:

Write the word:

Color the stars that have the word "**next**"

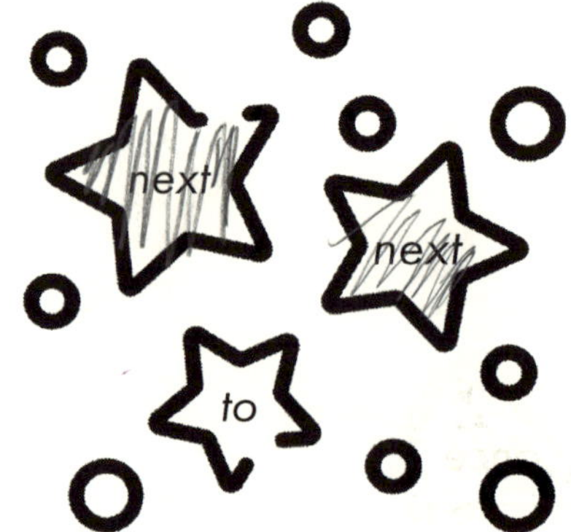

Let's work on our cutting and pasting skills. Cut out the word "**next**" from page 175 and paste it in the square box below to complete the sentence. Then read the sentence aloud!

My teacher retires [ ] year.

Write your own sentence using the word **next**:

I go to the dentist **once** a year.

Trace the word:

Write the word:

Color the pie pieces that have the word "**once**"

Find and circle the word "**once**"

u c j o d m
z y n w d c
u c b t v b
e d b r m b
u w v p s w
w m i n n a

Fill in the missing letters to make the word "**once**"

onc_ **on__**

____ **_n_e**

__ce **____**

I go to the dentist ____ a year.

Write your own sentence using the word **once**:

Banks **open** at eight o'clock.

Trace the word:

open

Write the word:

Color the pizza slices that have the word "**open**"

are he open open is me you open

Let's work on our cutting and pasting skills. Cut out the word "**open**" from page 175 and paste it in the square box below to complete the sentence. Then read the sentence aloud!

Banks [ ] at eight o'clock.

Write your own sentence using the word **open**:

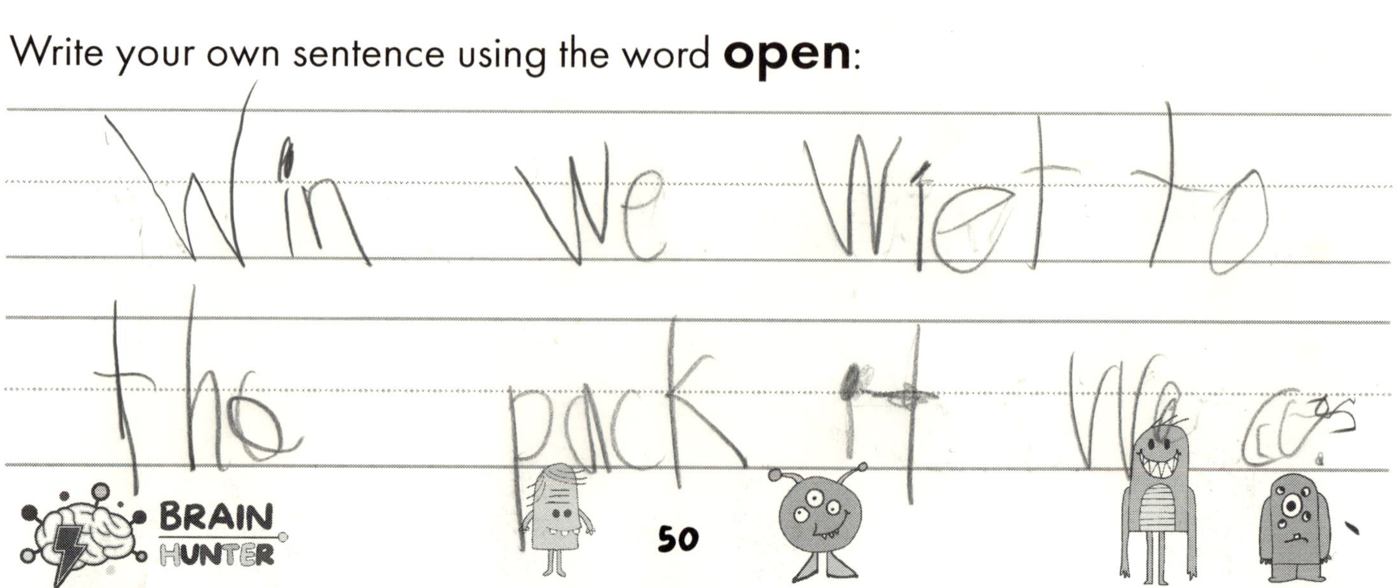

Is that a cat **or** a dog?

Trace the word:

Write the word:

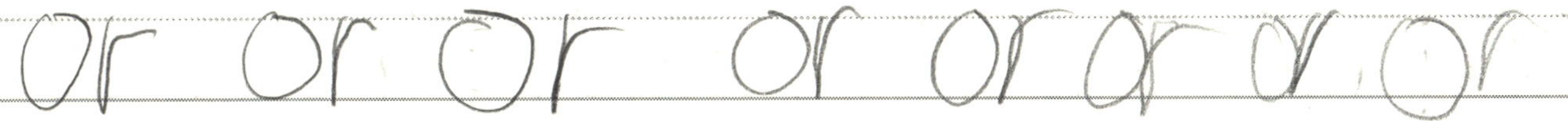

Color the puzzle pieces that have the word "**or**"

Find and circle the word "**or**"

d	i	i	u	l	v
r	a	o	s	f	k
c	b	r	b	y	i
y	b	e	c	q	g
g	l	d	f	a	i
a	n	o	x	d	a

Fill in the missing letters to make the word "**or**"

_r o_ __

__ o_ __

__ __ __

Is that a cat __ __ a dog?

Write your own sentence using the word **or**:

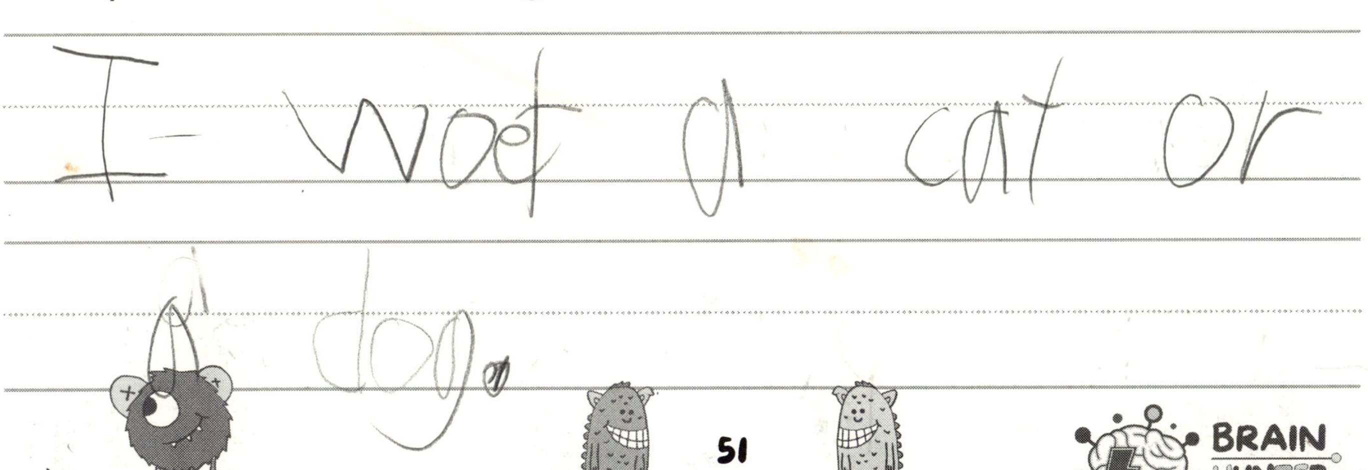

BRAIN HUNTER

John and Lucy are married to each **other.**

Trace the word:

other

Write the word:

Color the puzzle pieces that have the word "**other**"

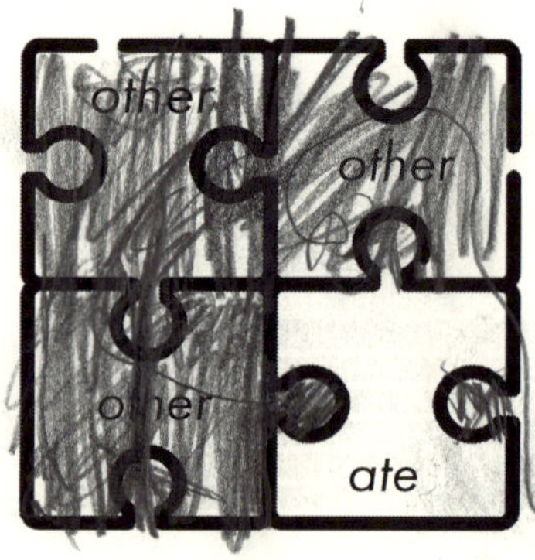

other other other ate

Let's work on our cutting and pasting skills. Cut out the word "**other**" from page 175 and paste it in the square box below to complete the sentence. Then read the sentence aloud!

John and Lucy are married each [ ] **.**

Write your own sentence using the word **other**:

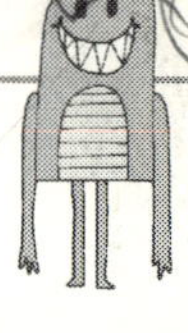

Welcome to **our** home.

Trace the word:

our our our

Write the word:

Color the pizza slices that have the word "**our**"	Find and circle the word "**our**"	Fill in the missing letters to make the word "**our**"

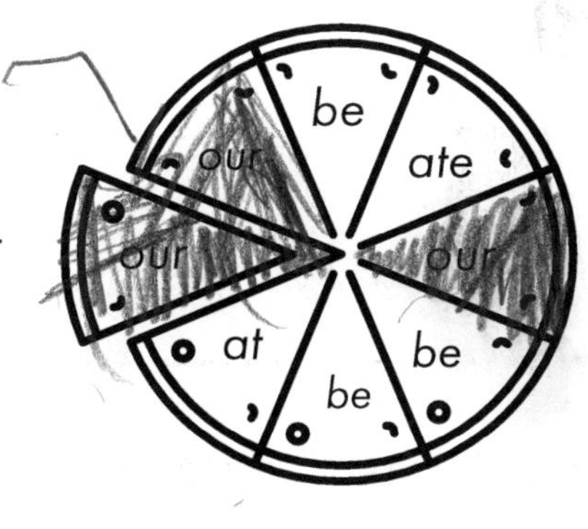

z n q v f w
s k g w r z
j a y a a g
y c v z o j
w k y e w l
s r u o m h

o_r **ou_**

_ _r **_u_**

_ _ _ **_ _ _**

Welcome to _ _ _ home.

Write your own sentence using the word **our**:

Matt **put** his luggage down.

Trace the word:

put

Write the word:

Color the stars that have the word "**put**"

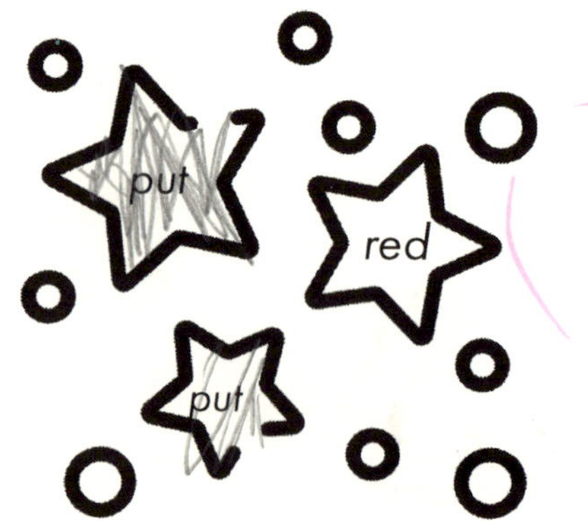

Let's work on our cutting and pasting skills. Cut out the word "**put**" from page 175 and paste it in the square box below to complete the sentence. Then read the sentence aloud!

Matt [ ] his luggage down.

Write your own sentence using the word **put**:

Slow and steady wins the **race**.

Trace the word:

Write the word:

Color the pie pieces that have the word "**race**"

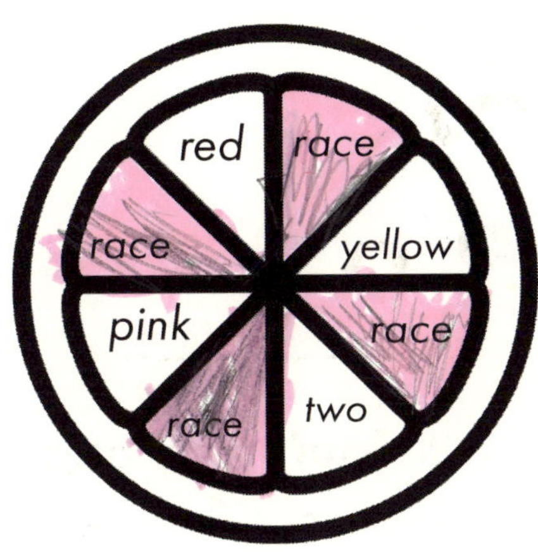

Find and circle the word "**race**"

n	d	k	k	p	a
s	u	q	m	v	m
r	s	y	p	y	i
m	a	f	p	y	c
x	y	c	x	p	s
x	e	k	e	r	k

Fill in the missing letters to make the word "**race**"

_ace   r_c_

_ _ce   _a_e

_ _ _e   _ _ _ _

Slow and steady wins the _ _ _ _.

Write your own sentence using the word **race**:

BRAIN HUNTER

Is it going to **rain** tomorrow?

Trace the word:

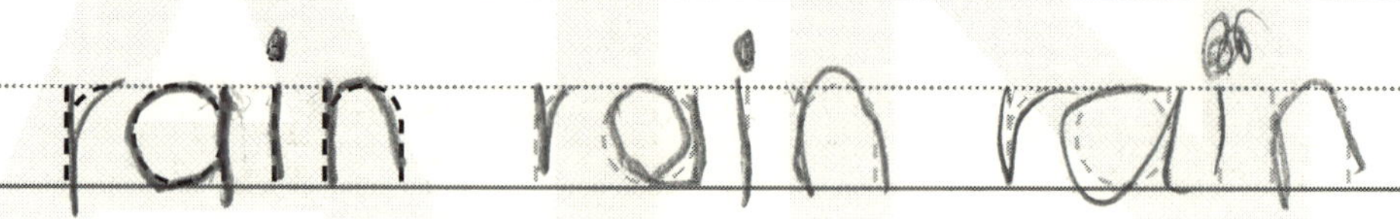

Write the word:

Color the pizza slices that have the word "**rain**"

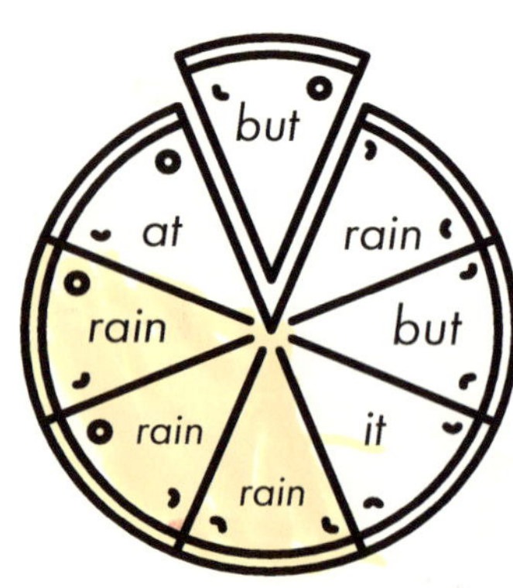

Let's work on our cutting and pasting skills. Cut out the word "**rain**" from page 175 and paste it in the square box below to complete the sentence. Then read the sentence aloud!

Is it going to  **tomorrow?**

Write your own sentence using the word **rain**:

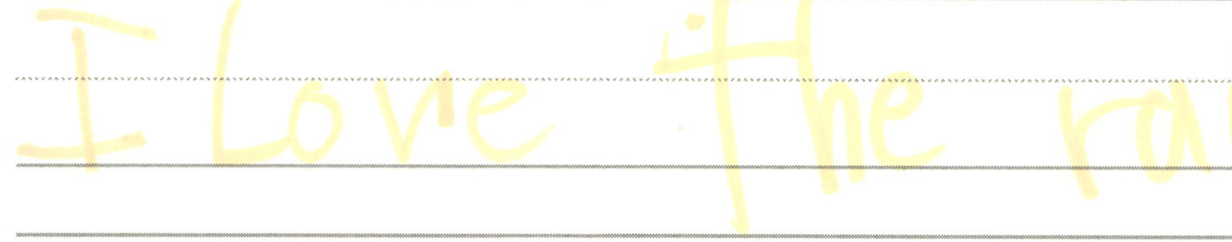

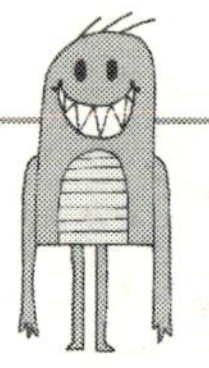

I like to **read** books everyday.

Trace the word:

read read read

Write the word:

Color the puzzle pieces that have the word "**read**"

Find and circle the word "**read**"

h	o	l	n	h	i
z	u	b	o	x	l
d	d	k	h	l	t
a	z	n	d	x	b
e	u	e	t	d	d
r	p	a	r	s	l

Fill in the missing letters to make the word "**read**"

_ead **r_a_**

__ad **_e_d**

____ **___d**

I like to ____ books every day.

Write your own sentence using the word **read**:

I **really** like playing basketball.

Trace the word:

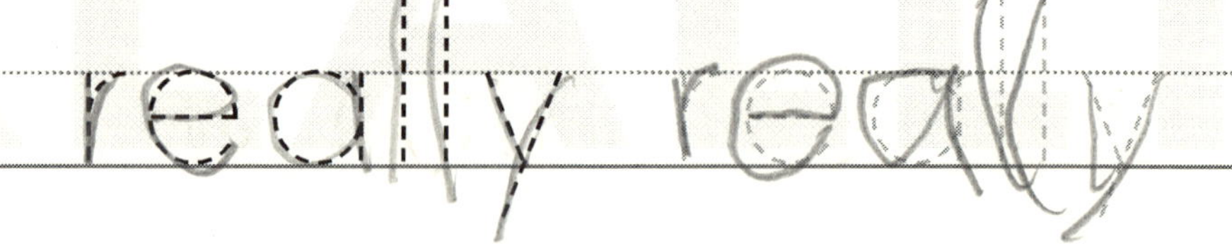

Write the word:

Color the puzzle pieces that have the word "**really**"

Let's work on our cutting and pasting skills. Cut out the word "**really**" from page 175 and paste it in the square box below to complete the sentence. Then read the sentence aloud!

I [ ] like playing basketball.

Write your own sentence using the word **really**:

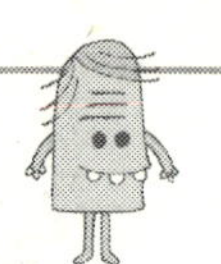

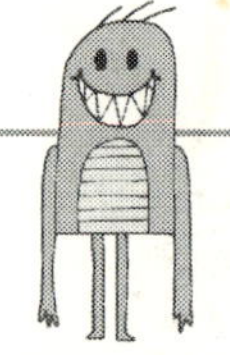

The earth is **round**.

Trace the word:

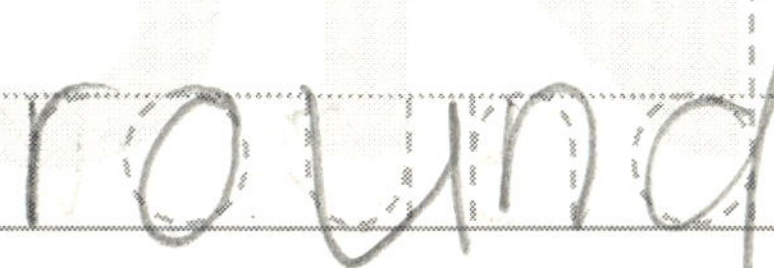

Write the word:

Color the pizza slices that have the word "**round**"

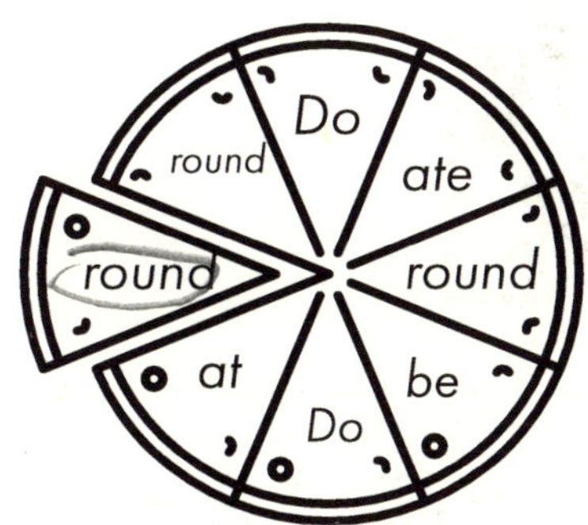

Find and circle the word "**round**"

e	c	z	u	w	y
b	e	a	v	o	g
f	j	y	n	i	d
i	j	b	n	t	o
m	n	i	m	c	v
r	o	u	n	d	z

Fill in the missing letters to make the word "**round**"

r_und **r_u_nd**

r__d **rou__**

__nd **_____**

The earth is _ _ _ _ _.

Write your own sentence using the word **round**:

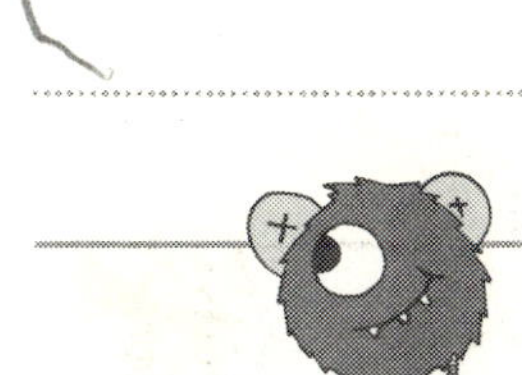

Christmas is coming **soon**.

Trace the word:

soon soon

Write the word:

soon soon soon

Color the stars that have the word "**soon**"

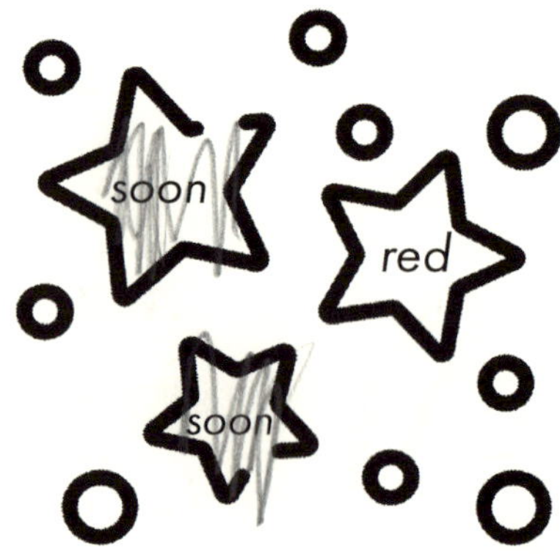

Let's work on our cutting and pasting skills. Cut out the word "**soon**" from page 175 and paste it in the square box below to complete the sentence. Then read the sentence aloud!

Christmas is coming soon **.**

Write your own sentence using the word **soon**:

I hope I can make brownies.

Julia is my **second** cousin.

Trace the word:

second second

Write the word:

Color the pie pieces that have the word "**second**"

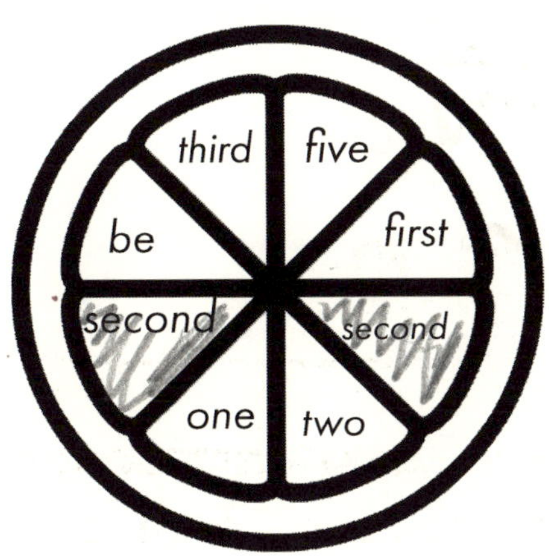

Find and circle the word "**second**"

n	a	s	l	m	m
k	f	s	l	x	z
s	e	c	o	n	d
d	i	y	c	e	j
v	q	e	p	p	i
r	x	p	s	i	l

Fill in the missing letters to make the word "**second**"

s _ _ ond _ e _ o _ d

sec _ _ d _ _ _ _ _ _

se _ o _ _ _ _ _ _ d

Julia is my _ _ _ _ _ _ cousin.

Write your own sentence using the word **second**:

I drank **seven** glasses of water today.

Trace the word:

seven

Write the word:

Color the pizza slices that have the word "**seven**"

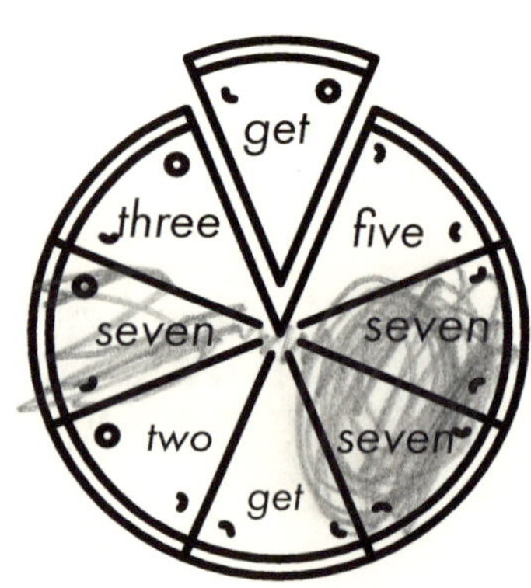

Let's work on our cutting and pasting skills. Cut out the word "**seven**" from page 175 and paste it in the square box below to complete the sentence. Then read the sentence aloud!

I drank [ ] glasses of water today.

Write your own sentence using the word **seven**:

It will soon be **spring**.

Trace the word:

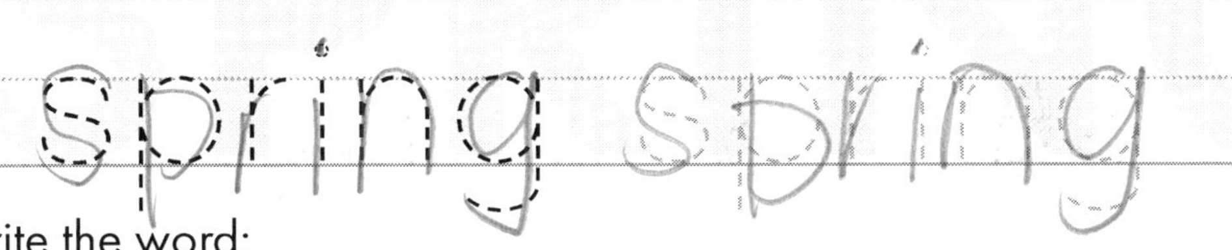

Write the word:

Color the puzzle pieces that have the word "**spring**"

Find and circle the word "**spring**"

g	z	w	i	i	k
h	n	b	l	k	t
l	c	i	d	p	c
w	e	w	r	n	i
r	y	z	f	p	o
t	f	l	f	a	s

Fill in the missing letters to make the word "**spring**"

__ring sp____

s_r_n_ ___ng

s____g ______

It will soon be ______.

Write your own sentence using the word **spring**:

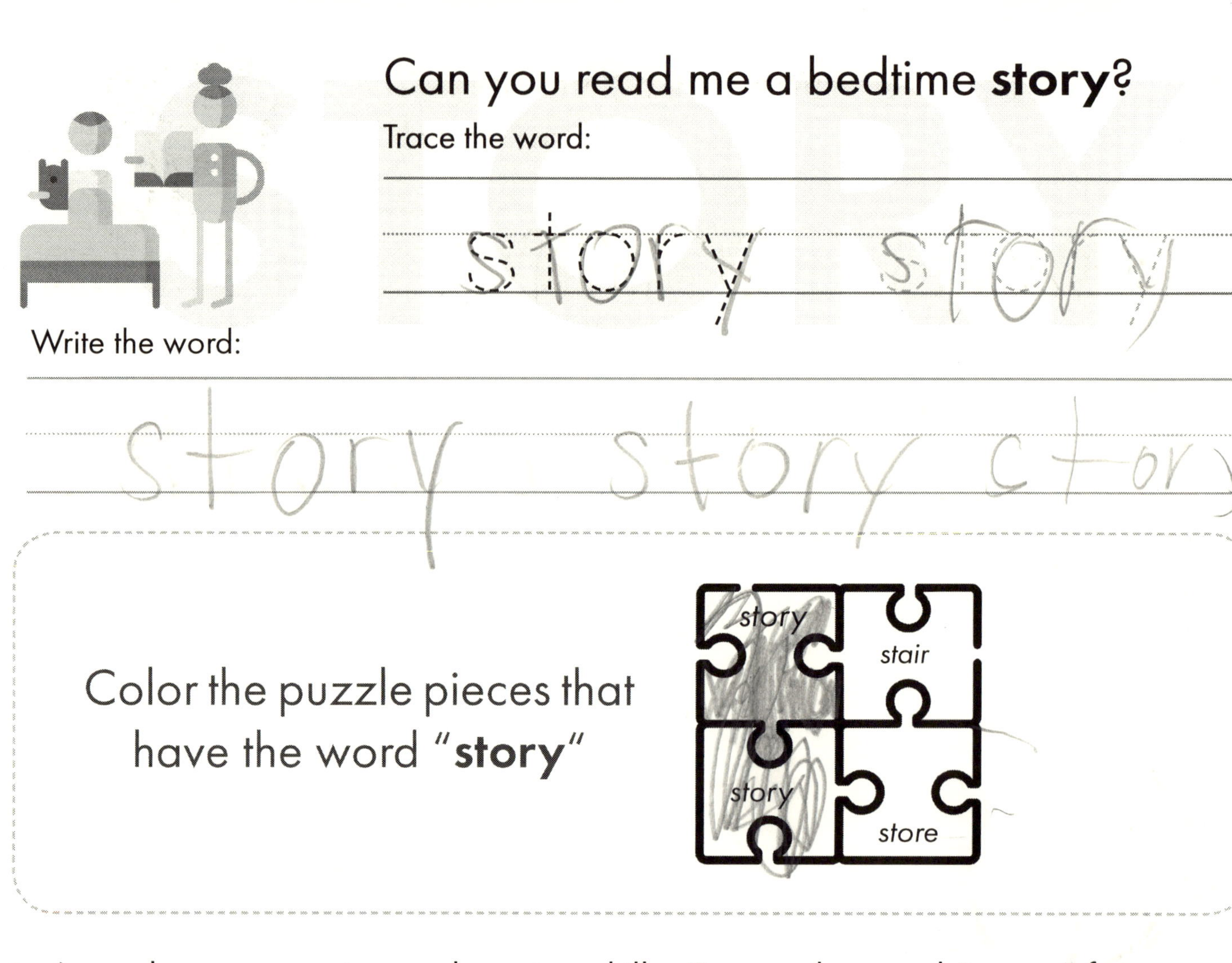

Can you read me a bedtime **story**?

Trace the word:

Write the word:

Color the puzzle pieces that have the word "**story**"

Let's work on our cutting and pasting skills. Cut out the word "**story**" from page 175 and paste it in the square box below to complete the sentence. Then read the sentence aloud!

Can you read me a bedtime [ ]?

Write your own sentence using the word **story**:

Why is everyone in **such** a hurry?

Trace the word:

such such

Write the word:

Color the pizza slices that have the word "**such**"

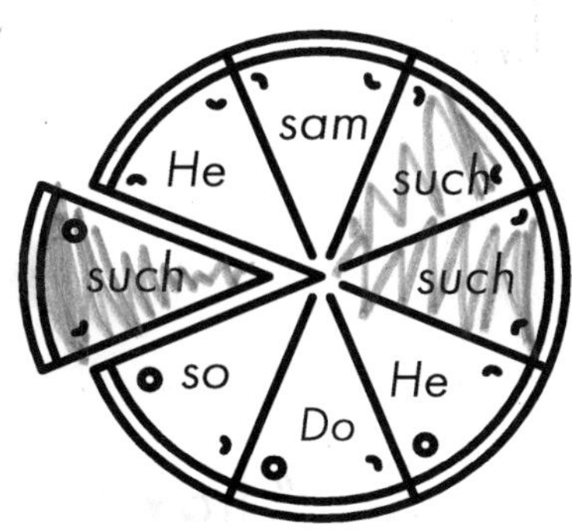

Find and circle the word "**such**"

i	j	d	d	e	m
s	c	m	t	c	l
f	u	s	c	z	d
q	q	c	z	t	b
r	x	c	h	z	g
g	x	g	q	w	a

Fill in the missing letters to make the word "**such**"

s_ch **su__**

s_c_ **___h**

suc_ **____**

Why is everyone in ____ a hury?

Write your own sentence using the word **such**:

Be **sure** to eat your vegetables everyday!

Trace the word:

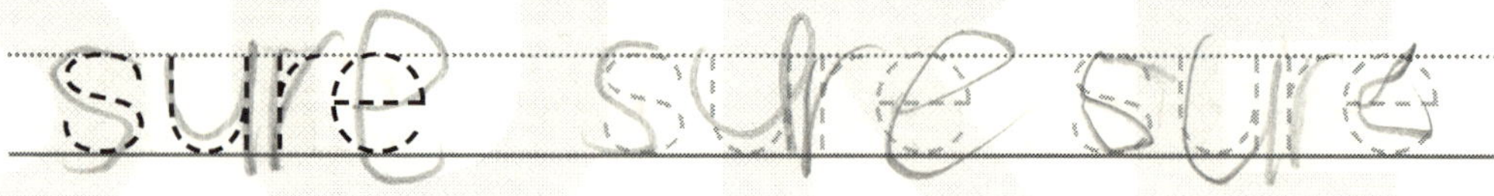

Write the word:

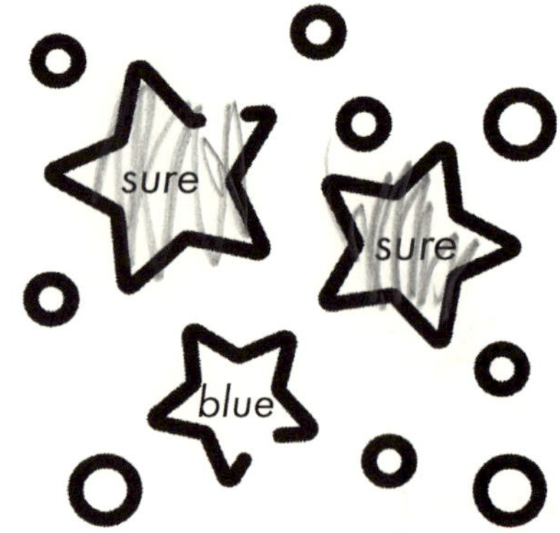

Color the stars that have the word "**sure**"

Let's work on our cutting and pasting skills. Cut out the word "**sure**" from page 175 and paste it in the square box below to complete the sentence. Then read the sentence aloud!

Be [ ] to eat your vegetables everyday.

Write your own sentence using the word **sure**:

That's a beautiful dress.

Trace the word:

That's

Write the word:

Color the pie pieces that have the word "**that's**"

Find and circle the word "**that's**"

e	h	z	u	t	p
o	w	b	h	b	o
a	i	a	f	j	z
o	t	m	v	b	j
s	l	i	w	j	k
w	d	z	k	m	r

Fill in the missing letters to make the word "**that's**"

___t's **th_t's**

t__t'_ **t_at's**

____'_ **____'s**

_ _ _ _ ' _ **a beautiful dress.**

Write your own sentence using the word **That's**:

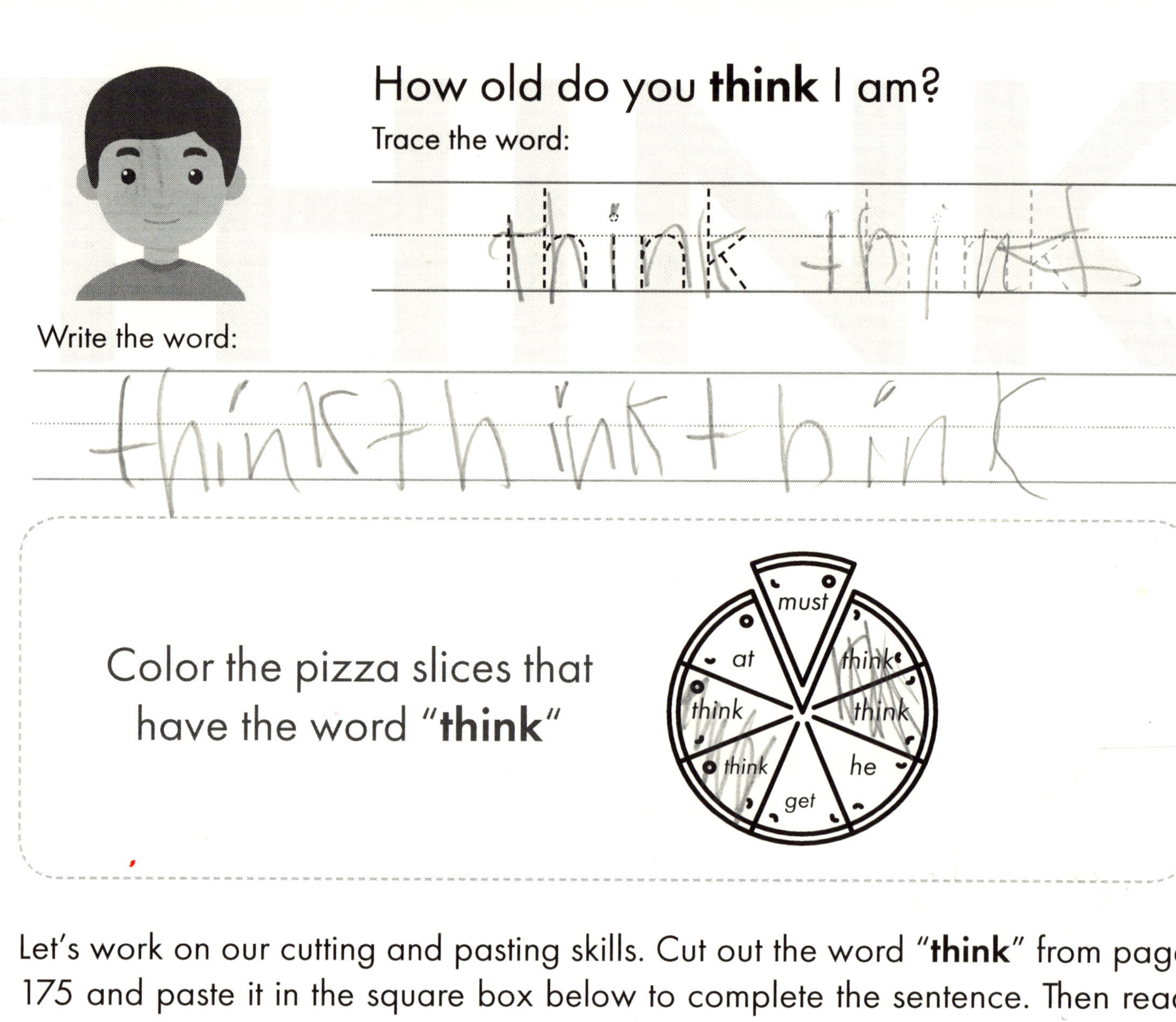

How old do you **think** I am?

Trace the word:

Write the word:

Color the pizza slices that have the word "**think**"

Let's work on our cutting and pasting skills. Cut out the word "**think**" from page 175 and paste it in the square box below to complete the sentence. Then read the sentence aloud!

How old do you [ ] I am?

Write your own sentence using the word **think**:

Those are my books.

Trace the word:

Those Those

Write the word:

Color the puzzle pieces that have the word "**those**"	Find and circle the word "**those**"	Fill in the missing letters to make the word "**those**"
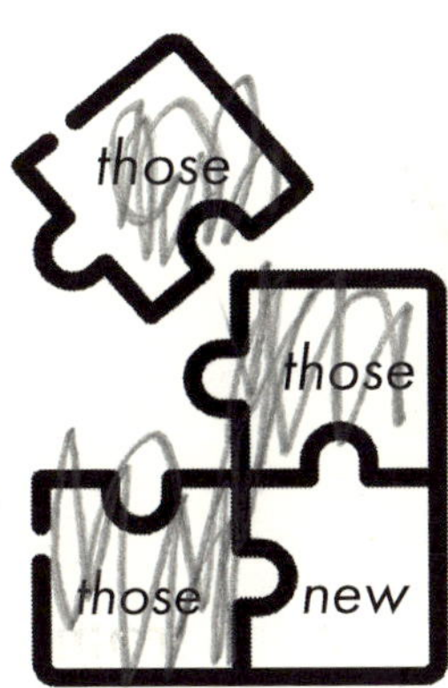	c m u e s b i m c s q t e s c o n s w n w h r a e u n t w v k g h t o n	___se th_se __o__ t___e _____ t____

_ _ _ _ _ **are my books.**

Write your own sentence using the word **those**:

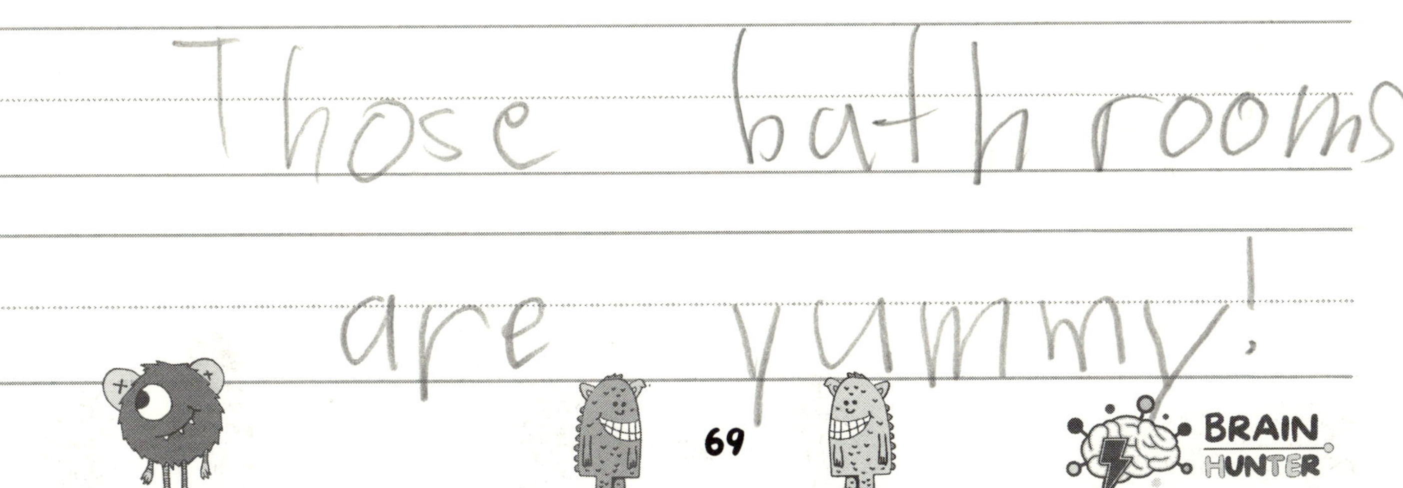

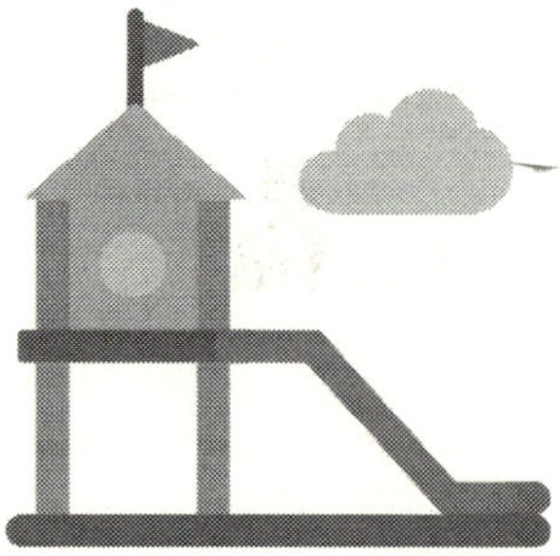

We had a really good **time**.

Trace the word:

time time

Write the word:

Color the puzzle pieces that have the word "**time**"

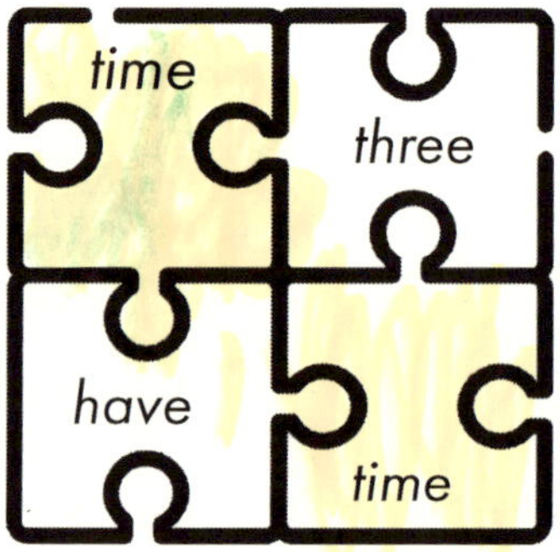

time three have time

Let's work on our cutting and pasting skills. Cut out the word "**time**" from page 175 and paste it in the square box below to complete the sentence. Then read the sentence aloud!

We had a really good ______.

Write your own sentence using the word **time**:

Is it going to rain **today**?

Trace the word:

today

Write the word:

Color the pizza slices that have the word "**today**"

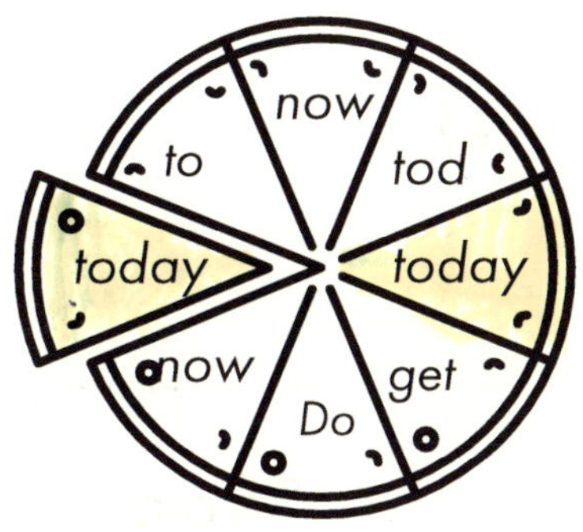

Find and circle the word "**today**"

y	o	d	b	l	b
l	a	o	t	d	r
a	e	d	n	w	n
s	y	p	o	p	u
d	e	u	v	t	m
y	f	n	t	e	m

Fill in the missing letters to make the word "**today**"

___ay to_ay

_o_a_ t___y

_____ t____

Is it going to rain _____?

Write your own sentence using the word **today**:

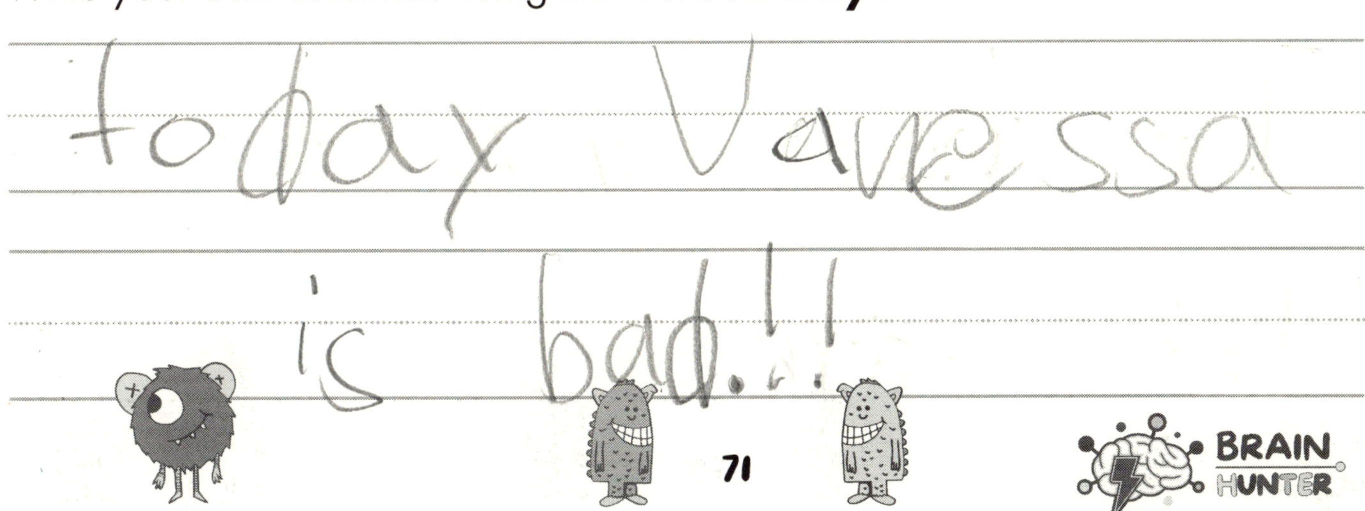

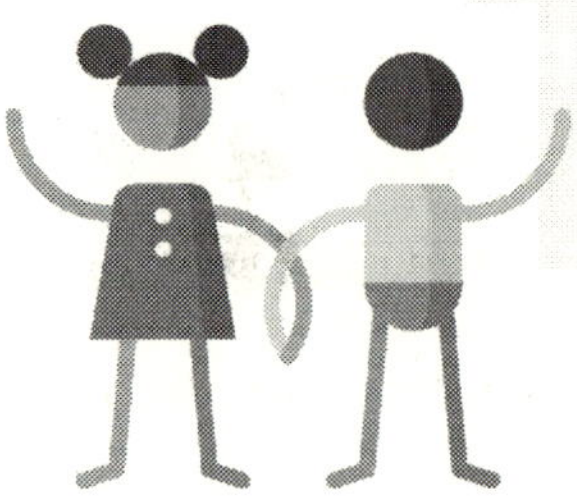

My friend and I go to school **together**.

Trace the word:

Write the word:

Color the star that has the word "**together**"

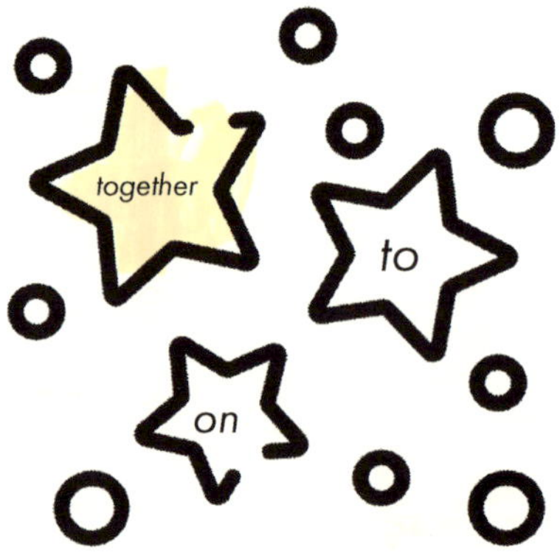

together

to

on

Let's work on our cutting and pasting skills. Cut out the word "**together**" from page 175 and paste it in the square box below to complete the sentence. Then read the sentence aloud!

My friend and I go to school ________ .

Write your own sentence using the word **together**:

This box is **too** heavy.

Trace the word:

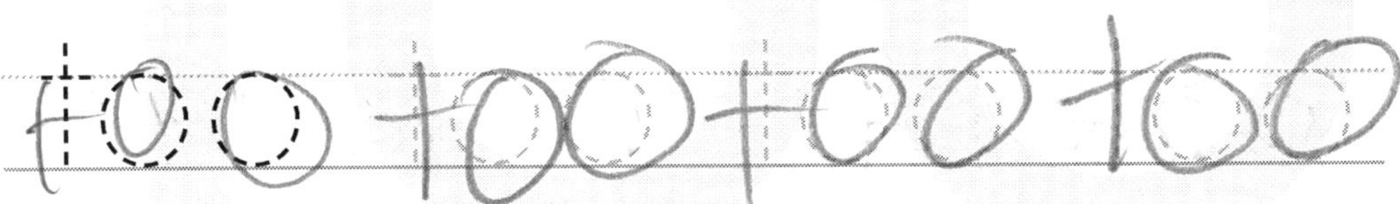

Write the word:

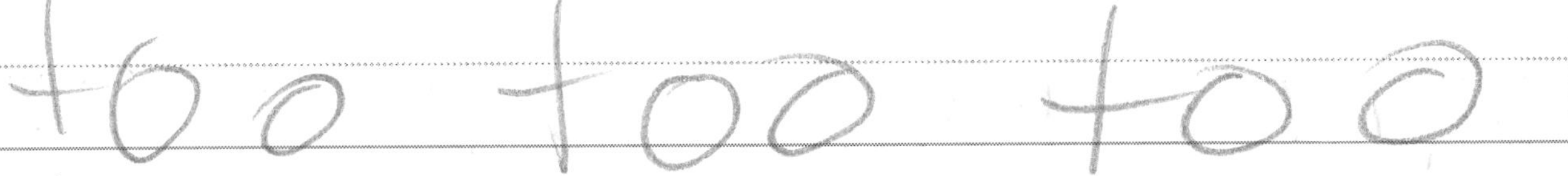

Color the pie pieces that have the word "**too**"

Find and circle the word "**too**"

e q j c w s
w t o o t v
i v t d n d
m k u i b r
g f s t y v
k n k h k r

Fill in the missing letters to make the word "**too**"

t_o   to_   _o

_o_   ___   ___

t__   ___   ___

This box is ___ heavy.

Write your own sentence using the word **too**:

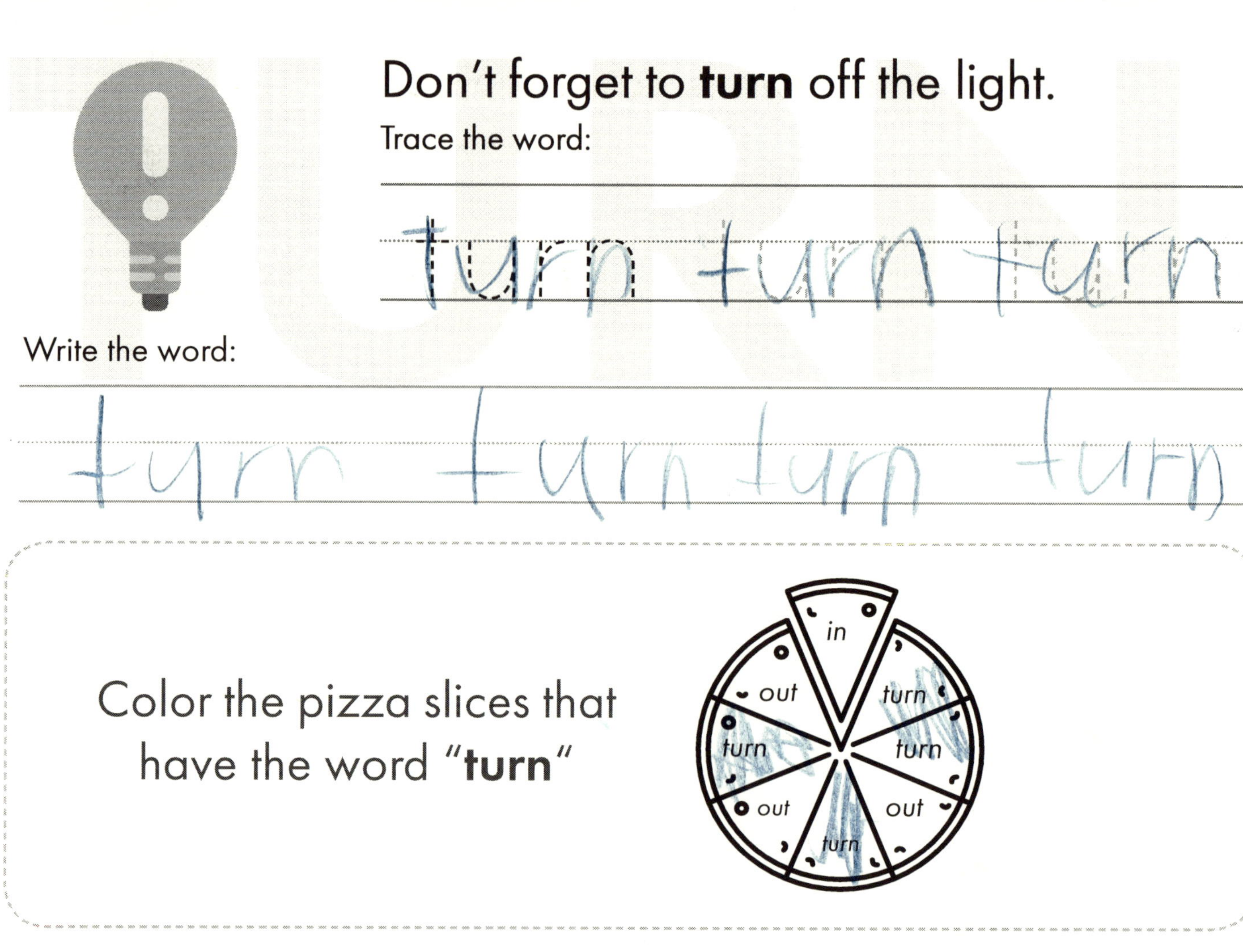

Don't forget to **turn** off the light.

Trace the word:

Write the word:

Color the pizza slices that have the word "**turn**"

Let's work on our cutting and pasting skills. Cut out the word "**turn**" from page 175 and paste it in the square box below to complete the sentence. Then read the sentence aloud!

Don't forget to [ ] off the light.

Write your own sentence using the word **turn**:

The **train** is now arriving.

Trace the word:

Write the word:

Color the puzzle pieces that have the word "**train**"

Find and circle the word "**train**"

n o p n m g
b i t d l h
s i a v i f
d p r r n k
o z o y t m
u j z y s a

Fill in the missing letters to make the word "**train**"

__ain   t_a_n

___in   _r_i_

t____   _____

The _ _ _ _ _ is now arriving.

Write your own sentence using the word **train**:

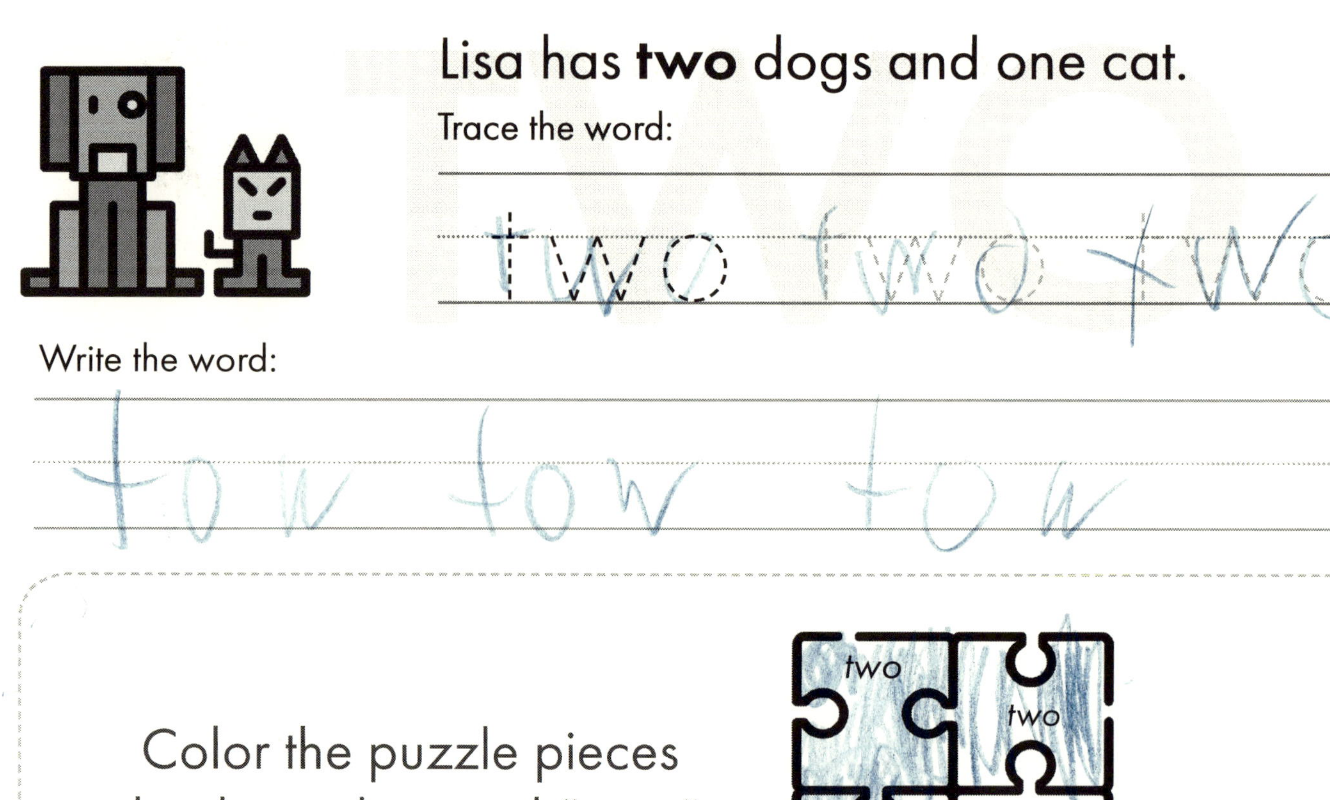

Lisa has **two** dogs and one cat.

Trace the word:

two two two

Write the word:

Color the puzzle pieces that have the word "**two**"

two
two
two
too

Let's work on our cutting and pasting skills. Cut out the word "**two**" from page 175 and paste it in the square box below to complete the sentence. Then read the sentence aloud!

Lisa has [ ] dogs and one cat.

Write your own sentence using the word **two**:

I **usually** walk to school.

Trace the word:

usually usually

Write the word:

Color the pizza slices that have the word "**usually**"

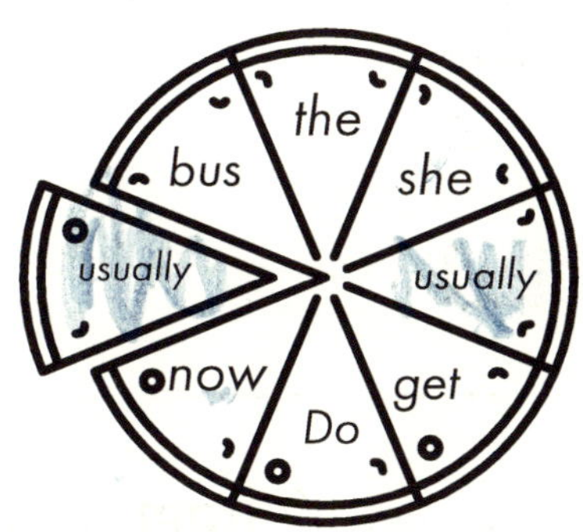

Find and circle the word "**usually**"

o	e	i	y	d	u	o
e	d	m	l	p	y	i
m	a	p	l	u	g	w
e	b	l	a	g	g	k
a	s	j	u	x	k	k
z	y	u	s	y	n	d
b	c	s	u	e	o	z

Fill in the missing letters to make the word "**usually**"

usua___ u_u_lly

u_____y ______y

us_a_l_ _______

I _______ walk to school.

Write your own sentence using the word **usually**:

I can’t **wait** to go on vacation.

Trace the word:

Write the word:

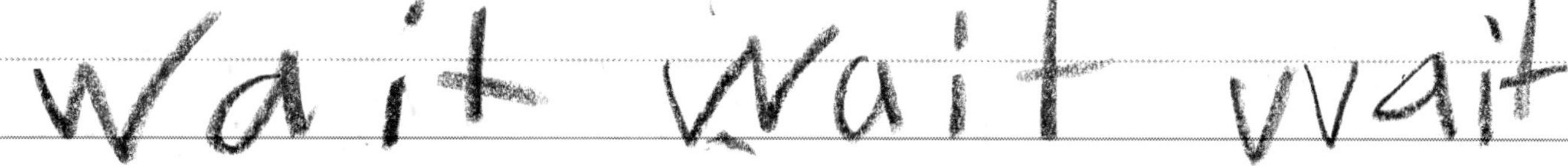

Color the stars that have the word “**wait**”

Let’s work on our cutting and pasting skills. Cut out the word “**wait**” from page 175 and paste it in the square box below to complete the sentence. Then read the sentence aloud!

I can’t ____ to go on vacation.

Write your own sentence using the word **wait**:

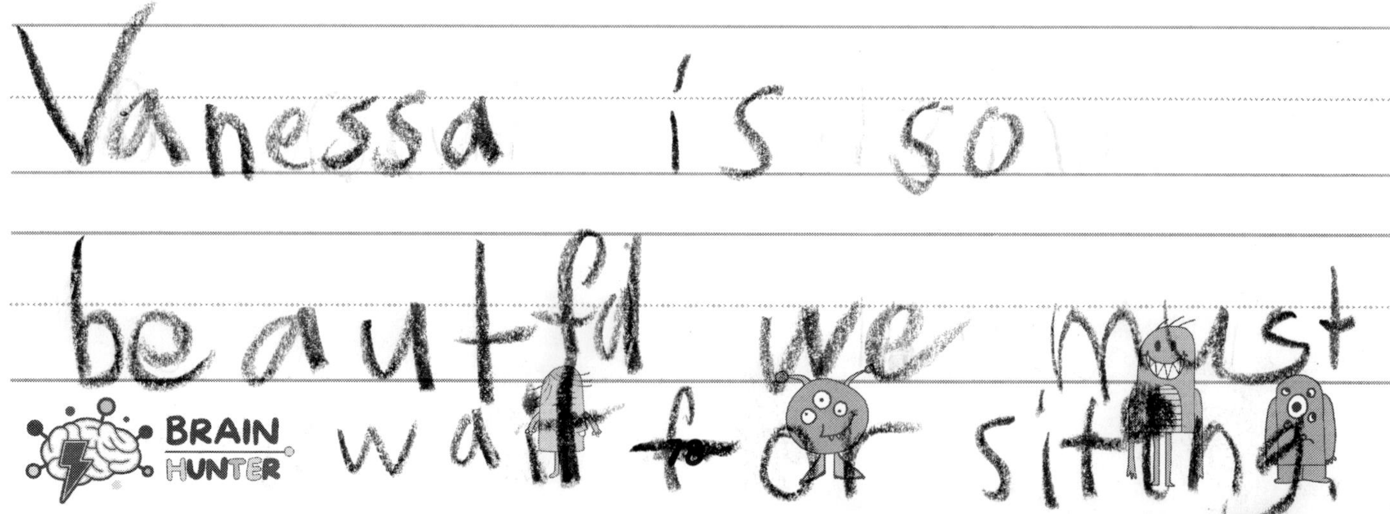

I **wish** I had a room of my own.

Trace the word:

Write the word:

Color the pie pieces that have the word "**wish**"

Find and circle the word "**wish**"

q	b	w	i	s	h
q	v	h	p	t	m
i	n	b	t	j	k
t	s	m	d	j	r
l	y	g	j	q	v
l	k	s	f	v	e

Fill in the missing letters to make the word "**wish**"

__sh **w_s_**

w__h **___h**

____ **wi__**

I ____ I had a room of my own.

Write your own sentence using the word **wish**:

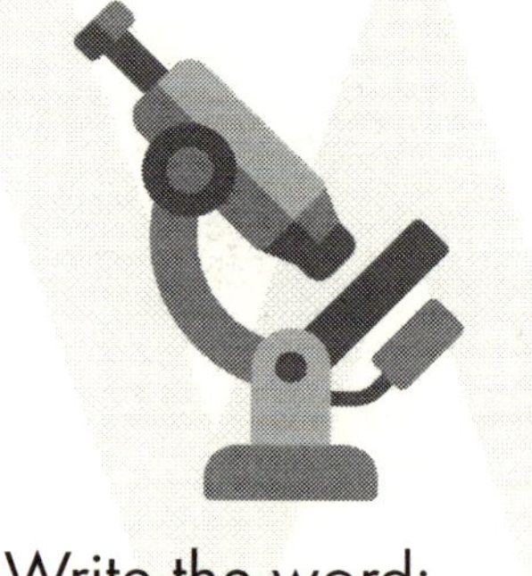

He **won** first place in the science fair.

Trace the word:

Write the word:

Color the pizza slices that have the word "**won**"

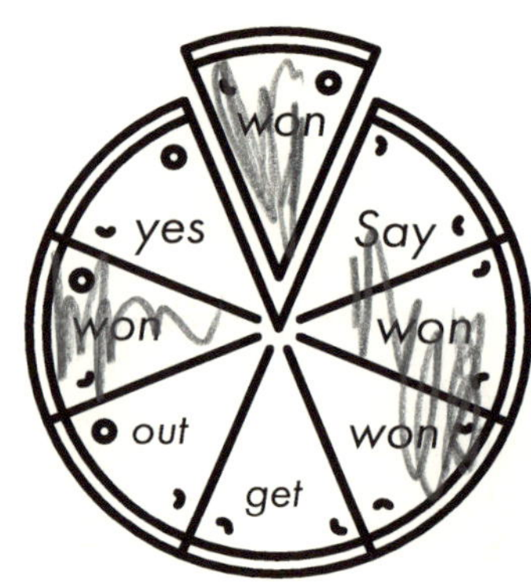

Let's work on our cutting and pasting skills. Cut out the word "**won**" from page 175 and paste it in the square box below to complete the sentence. Then read the sentence aloud!

He [ ] first place in the science fair!

Write your own sentence using the word **won**:

The car engine does not **work**.

Trace the word:

work work

Write the word:

Color the puzzle pieces that have the word "**work**"

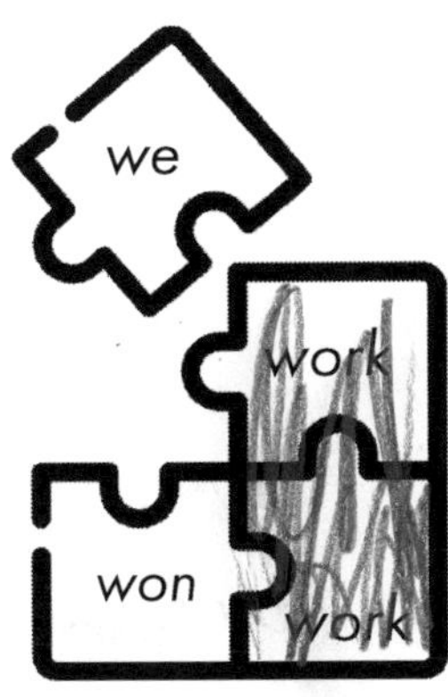

Find and circle the word "**work**"

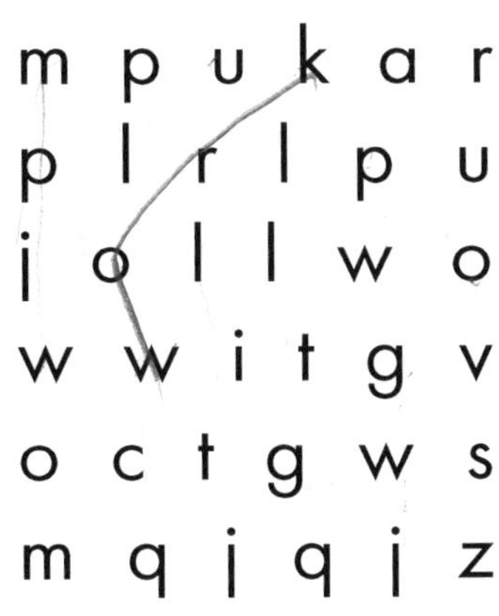

Fill in the missing letters to make the word "**work**"

__rk   w_r_

w__k   ___k

____   wo__

The car engine does not ____.

Write your own sentence using the word **work**:

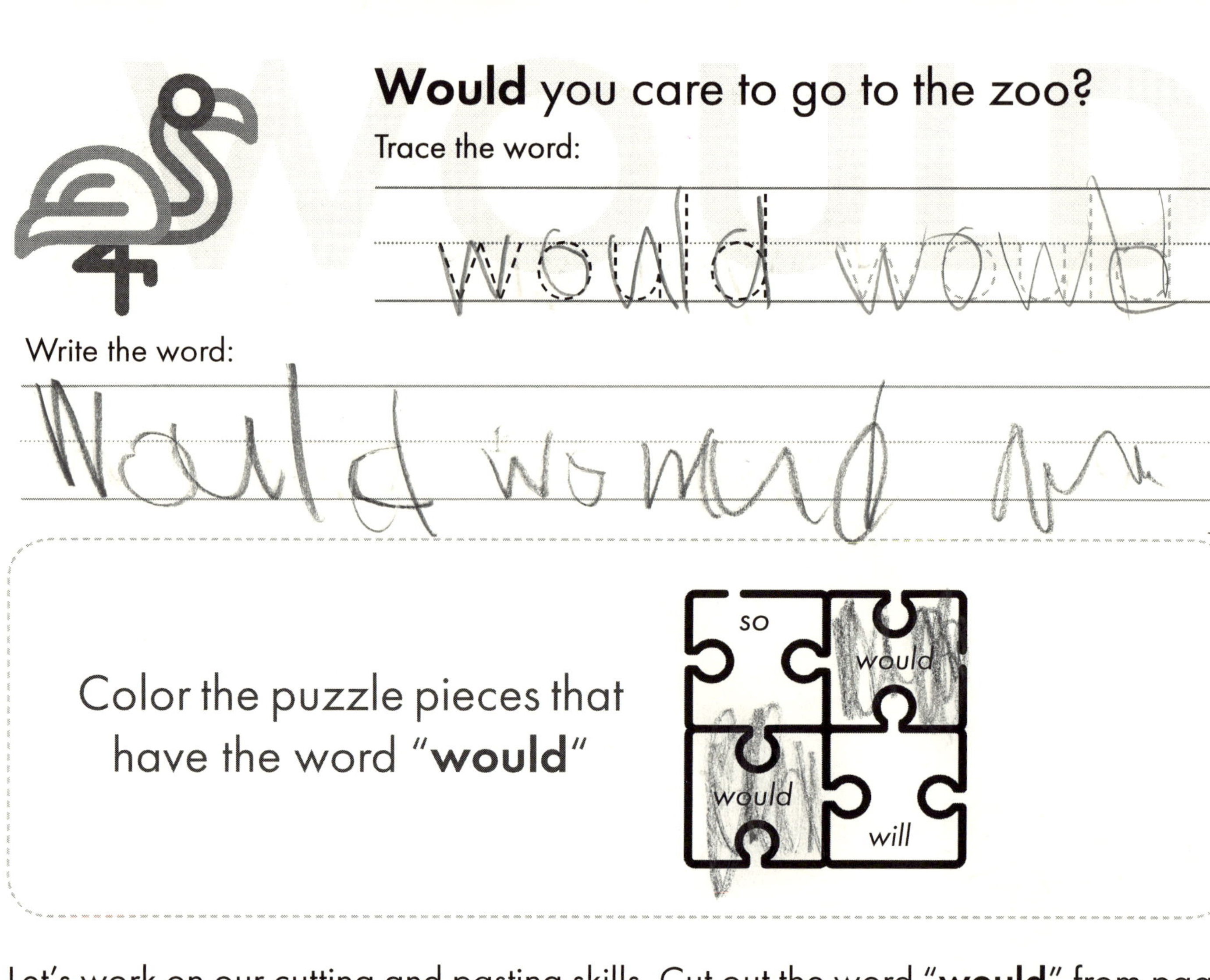

Would you care to go to the zoo?

Trace the word:

Write the word:

Color the puzzle pieces that have the word "**would**"

Let's work on our cutting and pasting skills. Cut out the word "**would**" from page 175 and paste it in the square box below to complete the sentence. Then read the sentence aloud!

[ ] you care to go to the zoo?

Write your own sentence using the word **would**:

The **wind** grew stronger.

Trace the word:

wind

Write the word:

Color the pizza slices that have the word "**wind**"

Find and circle the word "**wind**"

k e j w y x
n j o s h b
u n d n i w
r r v y y g
e w r w g f
d n m c u p

Fill in the missing letters to make the word "**wind**"

_ind **w_nd**

__nd **_i_d**

w__d **____**

The ____ grew stronger.

Write your own sentence using the word **wind**:

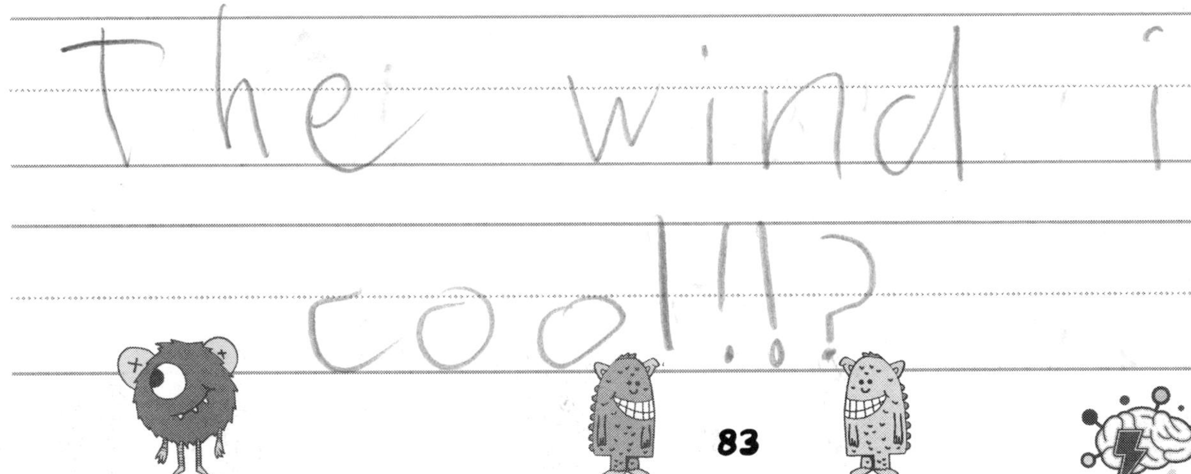

Come eat **with** us!

Trace the word:

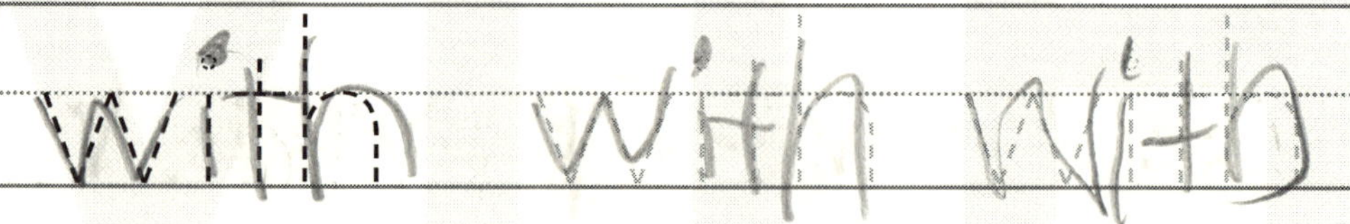

Write the word:

Color the stars that have the word "**with**"

Let's work on our cutting and pasting skills. Cut out the word "**with**" from page 175 and paste it in the square box below to complete the sentence. Then read the sentence aloud!

Come eat [ ] us.

Write your own sentence using the word **with**:

Chris went to Spain last **year**.

Trace the word:

year

Write the word:

Color the pie pieces that have the word "**year**"

Find and circle the word "**year**"

a n b y q r
y z e j d v
y a b p b j
r n j m h p
u m q r p n
n k j i x b

Fill in the missing letters to make the word "**year**"

_ear   y_a_

__ar   y_ar

_ea_   ____

Chris went to Spain last ____.

Write your own sentence using the word **year**:

I am **writing** a letter to my aunt.

Trace the word:

writing writing

Write the word:

Color the pizza slices that have the word "**writing**"

Let's work on our cutting and pasting skills. Cut out the word "**writing**" from page 175 and paste it in the square box below to complete the sentence. Then read the sentence aloud!

I am [ ] a letter to my aunt.

Write your own sentence using the word **writing**:

Bananas are **yellow.**

Trace the word:

yellow yellow

Write the word:

Color the puzzle pieces that have the word "**yellow**"

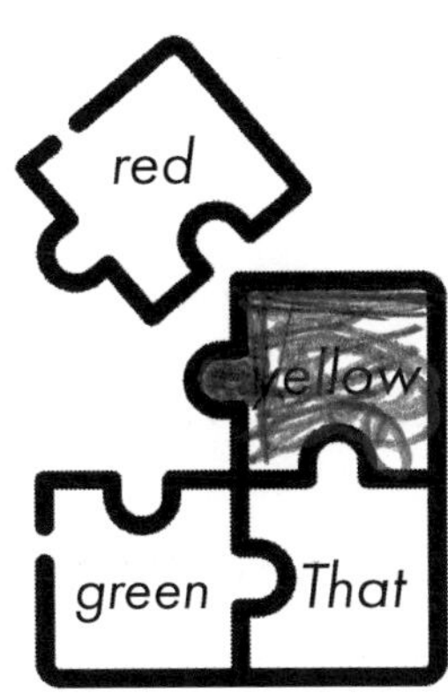

Find and circle the word "**yellow**"

s v j q z w
u e f p o g
j l t l n n
e e l n x g
u e p e b n
y z o s n h

Fill in the missing letters to make the word "**yellow**"

__llow **ye__ow**

___ow **y___w**

_e__o_ **yel___**

Bananas are ______.

Write your own sentence using the word **yellow**:

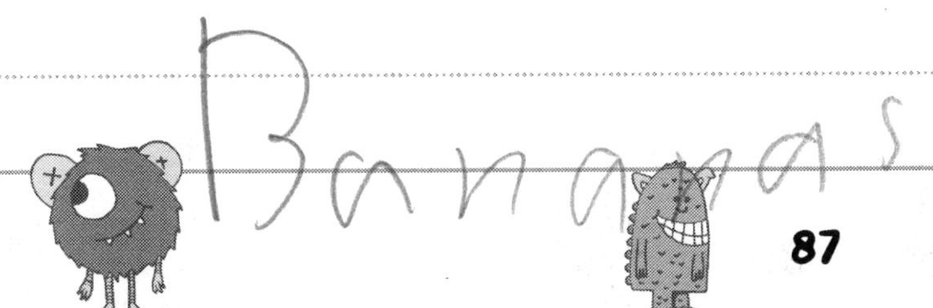

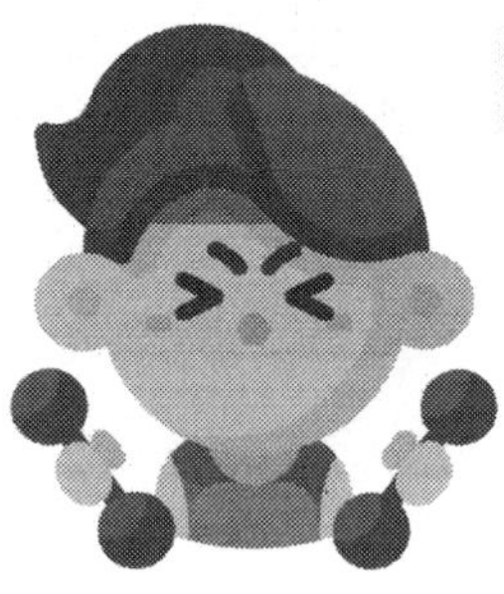

I am **too** tired to exercise.

Trace the word:

too too too

Write the word:

too too too too

Color the puzzle pieces that have the word "**too**"

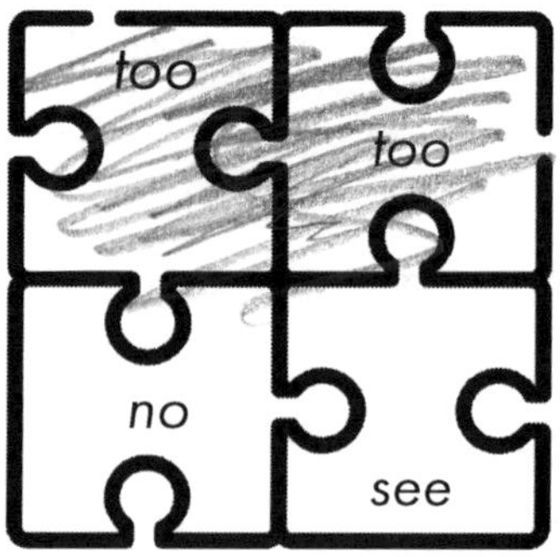

Let's work on our cutting and pasting skills. Cut out the word "**too**" from page 175 and paste it in the square box below to complete the sentence. Then read the sentence aloud!

I am too **tired to exercise.**

Write your own sentence using the word **too**:

I Love pupes my sisten like then too

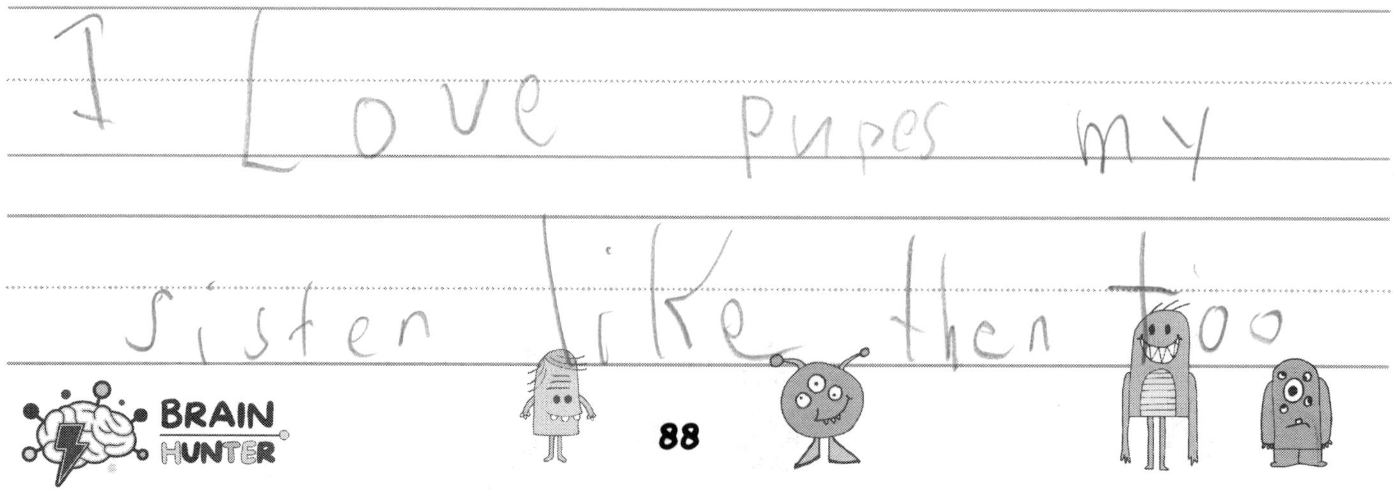

The pencil is **under** the table.

Trace the word:

under under

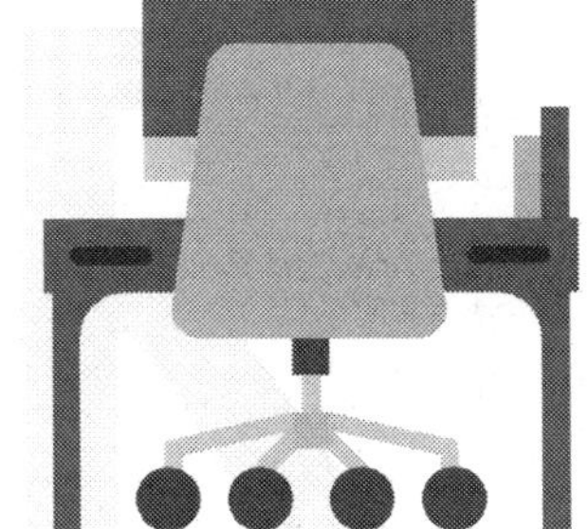

Write the word:

Color the pizza slices that have the word "**under**"

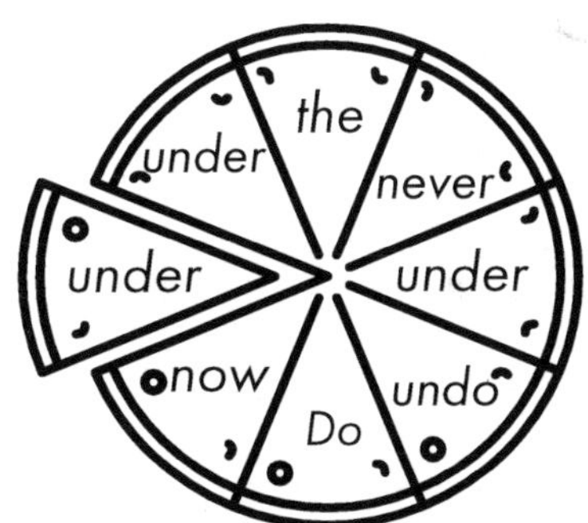

Find and circle the word "**under**"

e	y	c	k	r	v
o	b	u	l	y	u
f	t	q	g	u	n
m	g	e	z	h	d
a	u	n	t	n	e
w	f	i	e	d	r

Fill in the missing letters to make the word "**under**"

_nder u_d_r

___er _n_e_

u__e_ _____

The pencil is _____ the table.

Write your own sentence using the word **under**:

Tom is **afraid** of spiders.

Trace the word:

afraid afraid

Write the word:

Color the pizza slices that have the word "**afraid**"

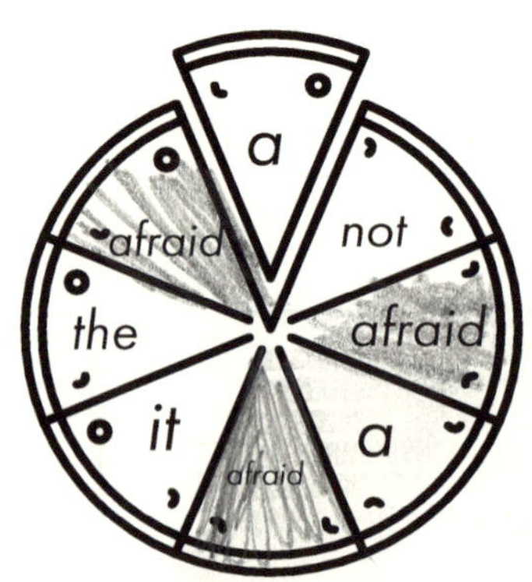

Let's work on our cutting and pasting skills. Cut out the letter "**afraid**" from page 175 and paste it in the square box below to complete the sentence. Then read the sentence aloud!

Tom is ______ of spiders.

Write your own sentence using the word **afraid**:

We **almost** won the soccer game.

Trace the word:

almost

Write the word:

Color the puzzle pieces that have the word "**almost**"

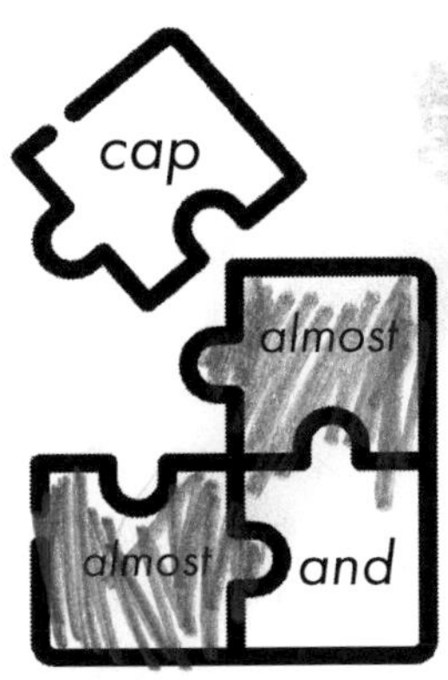

Find and circle the word "**almost**"

r	q	b	l	h	a
z	l	c	e	l	b
g	v	o	m	e	g
z	w	o	g	q	n
m	s	x	c	z	c
t	k	z	s	y	a

Fill in the missing letters to make the word "**almost**"

a _ _ _ st **al _ _ _ _**

_ _ _ _ _ t **_ _ m _ _ _**

_ l _ _ _ t **_ _ _ _ _ _**

We _ _ _ _ _ _ won the soccer game.

Write your own sentence using the word **almost**:

I **always** try my best.

Trace the word:

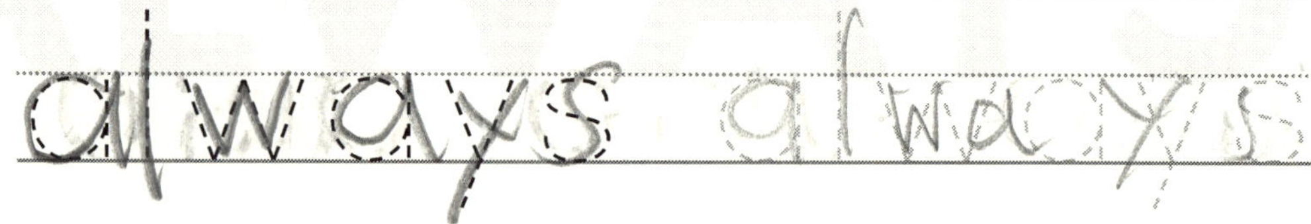

Write the word:

always always always

Color the puzzle pieces that have the word "**always**"

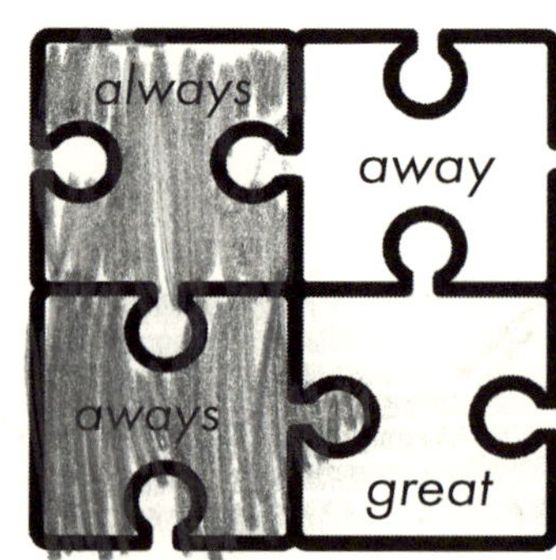

Let's work on our cutting and pasting skills. Cut out the word "**always**" from page 175 and paste it in the square box below to complete the sentence. Then read the sentence aloud!

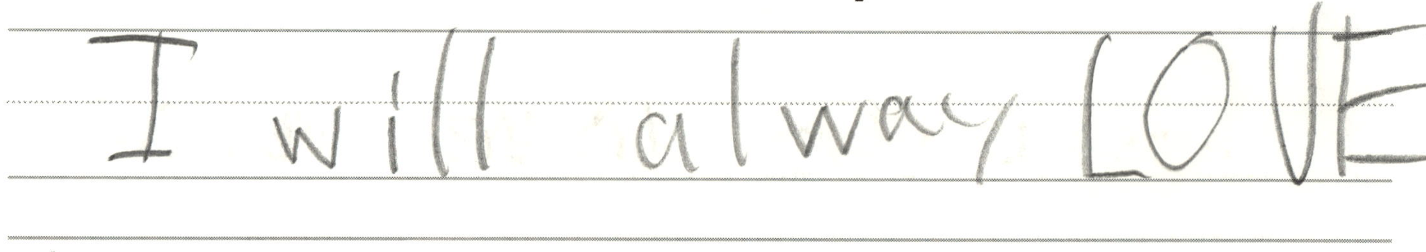

Write your own sentence using the word **always**:

I will alway LOVE horses.

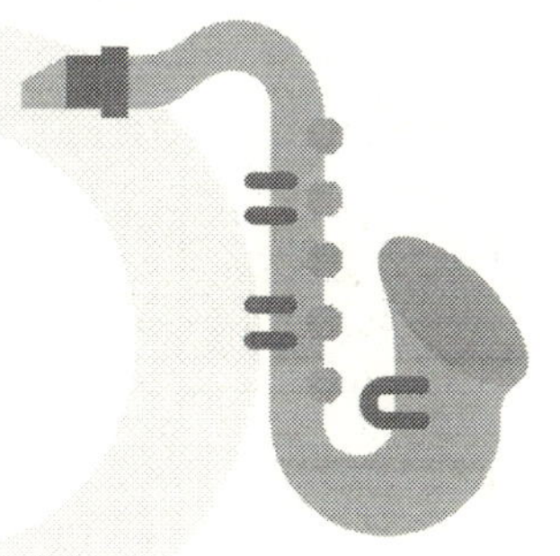

Do you **also** like jazz?

Trace the word:

Write the word:

Color the pizza slices that have the word "**also**"

Find and circle the word "**also**"

a	n	a	h	k	e
j	f	q	l	s	h
g	l	z	s	s	k
t	x	n	m	h	o
e	d	k	j	v	d
x	u	y	t	j	n

Fill in the missing letters to make the word "**also**"

al__   **als_**

___o   **a_s_**

a___   **____**

Do you ____ like jazz?

Write your own sentence using the word **also**:

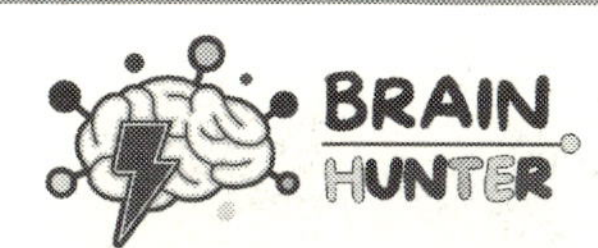

What is your favorite **animal**?

Trace the word:

animal animal

Write the word:

Color the stars that have the word "**animal**"

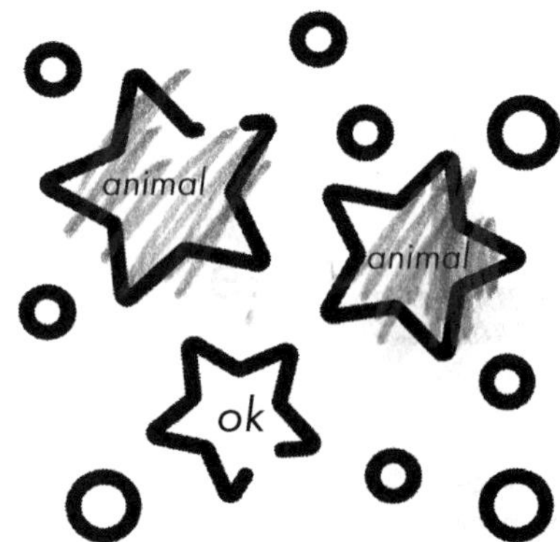

Let's work on our cutting and pasting skills. Cut out the word "**animal**" from page 175 and paste it in the square box below to complete the sentence. Then read the sentence aloud!

What is your favorite [ ]?

Write your own sentence using the word **animal**:

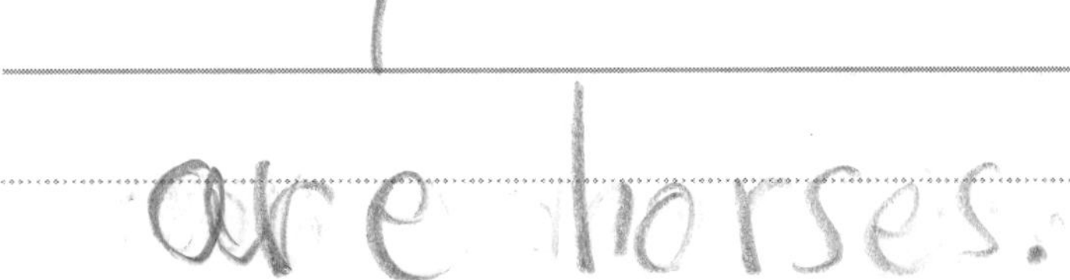

Can **anyone** help me?

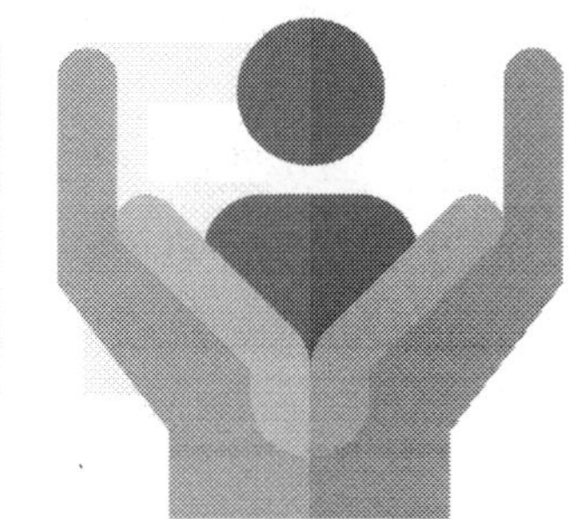

Trace the word:

anyone anyone

Write the word:

Color the pie pieces that have the word "**anyone**"	Find and circle the word "**anyone**"	Fill in the missing letters to make the word "**anyone**"
		___one any___ _n_o__ a____e a_____ ______

Can ______ help me?

Write your own sentence using the word **anyone**:

BRAIN HUNTER

Mary wants to **become** a doctor.

Trace the word:

become

Write the word:

Color the pizza slices that have the word "**become**"

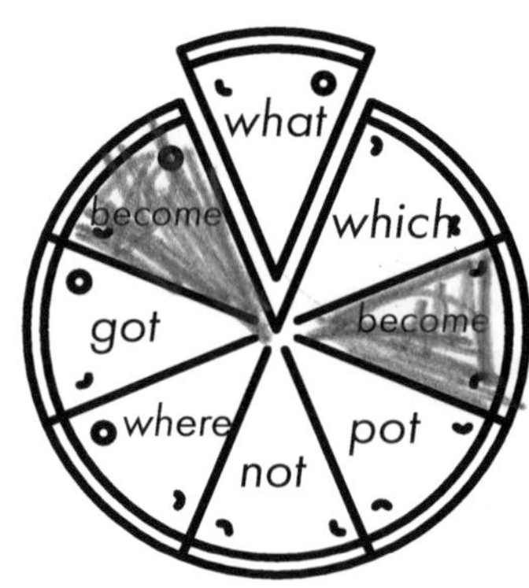

Let's work on our cutting and pasting skills. Cut out the word "**become**" from page 177 and paste it in the square box below to complete the sentence. Then read the sentence aloud!

Mary wants to ______ a doctor.

Write your own sentence using the word **become**:

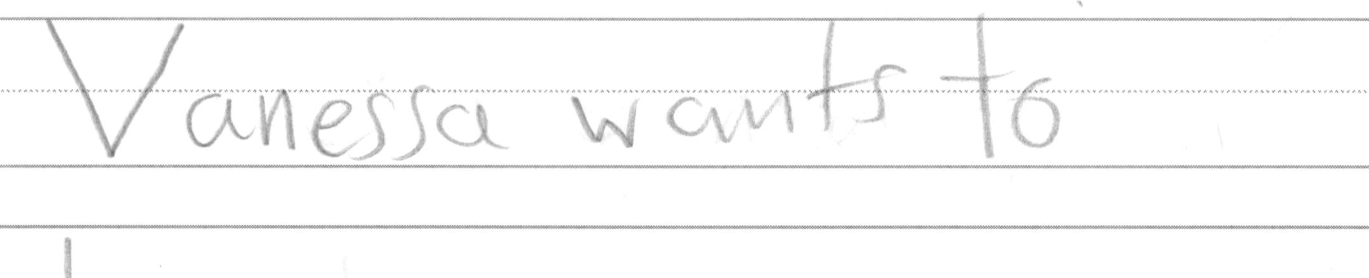

My dad will be **away** for a week.

Trace the word:

away away

Write the word:

Color the puzzle pieces that have the word "**away**"

Find and circle the word "**away**"

s	g	a	c	v	a
v	h	g	p	j	h
p	u	o	j	s	g
a	c	j	u	z	g
o	y	w	d	l	m
p	q	r	u	i	d

Fill in the missing letters to make the word "**away**"

aw_ _ **a_ _y**

a_a_ **_ _ _y**

a_ _ _ **_ _ _ _**

My dad will be _ _ _ _ for a week.

Write your own sentence using the word **away**:

I don't **know** her name.

Trace the word:

know know know

Write the word:

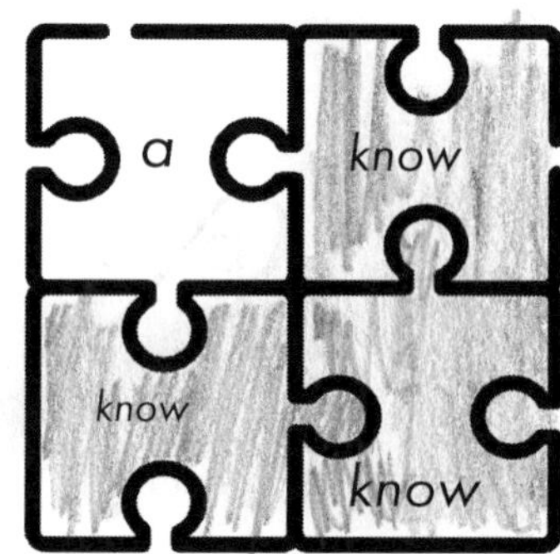

Color the puzzle pieces that have the word "**know**"

Let's work on our cutting and pasting skills. Cut out the word "**know**" from page 177 and paste it in the square box below to complete the sentence. Then read the sentence aloud!

I don't [ ] her name.

Write your own sentence using the word **know**:

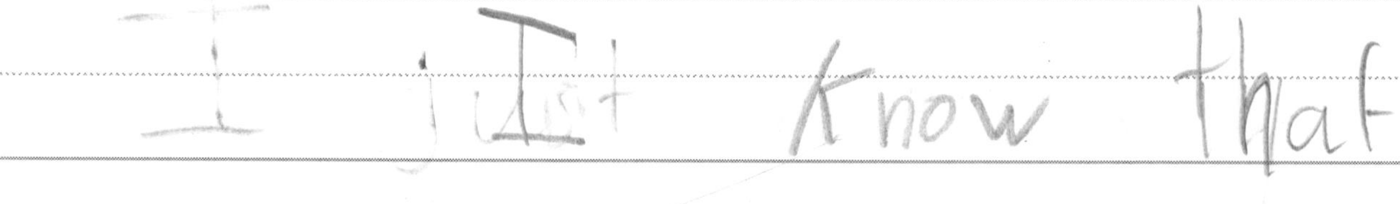

Always **believe** in yourself!

Trace the word:

believe believe

Write the word:

Color the pizza slices that have the word "**believe**"

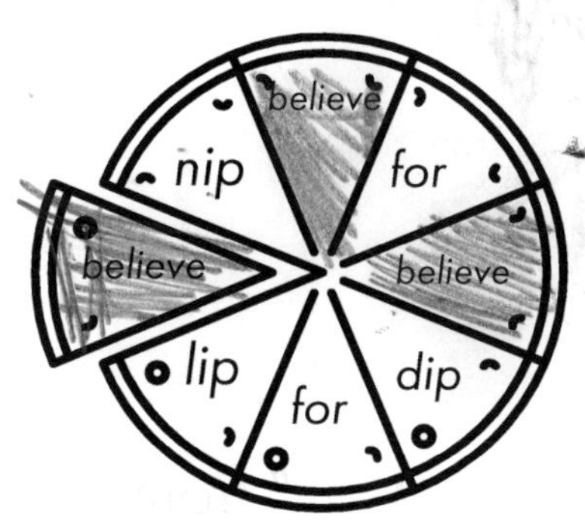

Find and circle the word "**believe**"

b	o	h	i	l	g	m
l	e	f	v	l	o	x
s	c	l	u	x	c	z
i	y	c	i	t	z	i
e	c	m	j	e	t	u
j	z	c	a	y	v	y
p	x	n	s	x	l	e

Fill in the missing letters to make the word "**believe**"

_e_i__e ______e

bel____ be_____

b______ _______

Always _ _ _ _ _ _ _ in yourself!

Write your own sentence using the word **believe**:

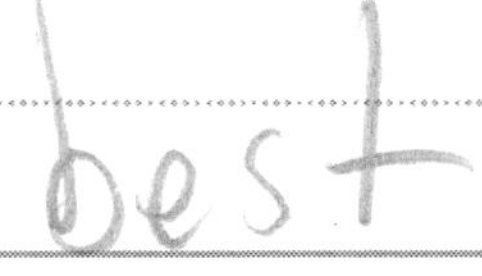

He **swims** better than I do.

Trace the word:

swims swims

Write the word:

Color the stars that have the word "**swims**"

Let's work on our cutting and pasting skills. Cut out the word "**swims**" from page 177 and paste it in the square box below to complete the sentence. Then read the sentence aloud!

He [ ] better than I do.

Write your own sentence using the word **swims**:

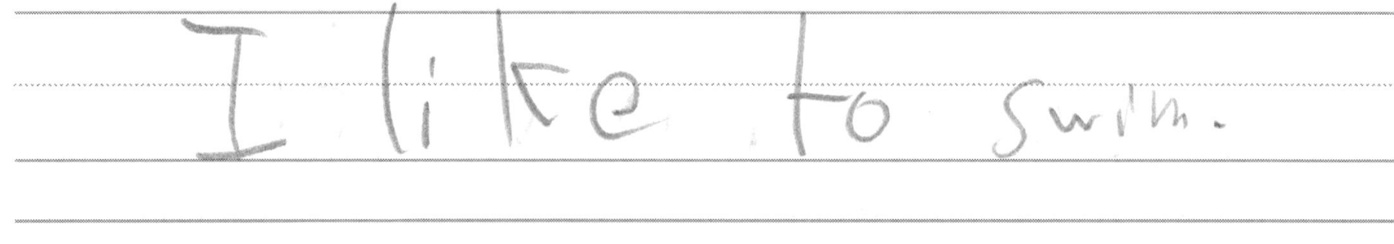

Let's **build** a snowman!

Trace the word:

build build

Write the word:

build build

Color the pie pieces that have the word "**build**"

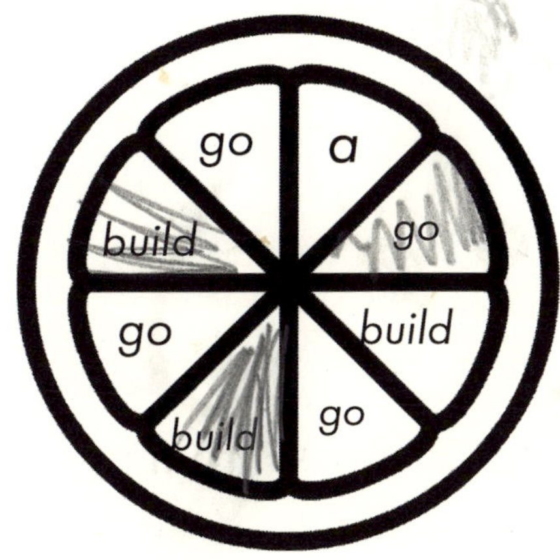

Find and circle the word "**build**"

g q v x v x
k i f s f p
w y i u n g
b u i l d v
q q n r j m
t r n b g v

Fill in the missing letters to make the word "**build**"

__ __ild **bu__ __ __**

__ __ __ld **b__il__**

b__ __ __ __ **__ __ __ __ __**

Let's __ __ __ __ __ a snowman!

Write your own sentence using the word **build**:

I don't **care** for eggs.

Trace the word:

care care care

Write the word:

care care care care

Color the pizza slices that have the word "**care**"

Let's work on our cutting and pasting skills. Cut out the word "**care**" from page 177 and paste it in the square box below to complete the sentence. Then read the sentence aloud!

I don't care for eggs.

Write your own sentence using the word **care**:

I care for horses.

Lisa wants to **buy** a new car.

Trace the word:

buy buy buy

Write the word:

buy buy buy buy

Color the puzzle pieces that have the word "**buy**"

Find and circle the word "**buy**"

b x y h z g
b u u m f d
t y y u v u
v j k h x q
o n m j h r
b x g h c o

Fill in the missing letters to make the word "**buy**"

b _ _   _ _ y

_ u _   _ _ _

_ _ _   _ _ _

Lisa wants to _ _ _ a new car.

Write your own sentence using the word **buy**:

I buy toys.

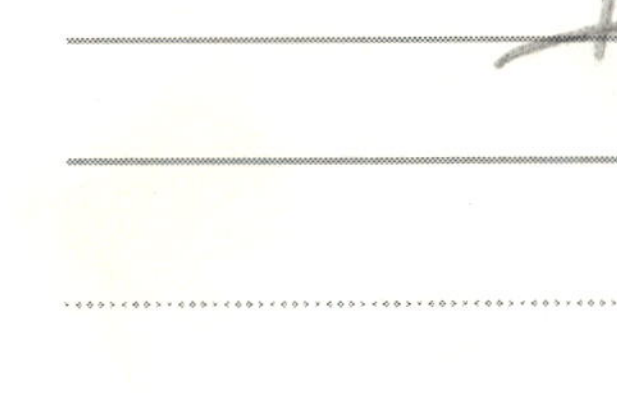

I need to wash my **clothes**.

Trace the word:

clothes clothes

Write the word:

Color the puzzle pieces that have the word "**clothes**"

Let's work on our cutting and pasting skills. Cut out the word "**clothes**" from page 177 and paste it in the square box below to complete the sentence. Then read the sentence aloud!

I need to wash my [ ] **.**

Write your own sentence using the word **clothes**:

We **caught** a big fish on our trip.

Trace the word:

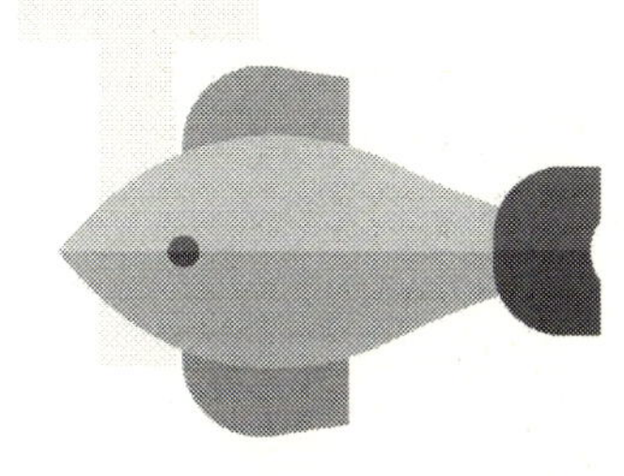

caught caught

Write the word:

Color the pizza slices that have the word "**caught**"

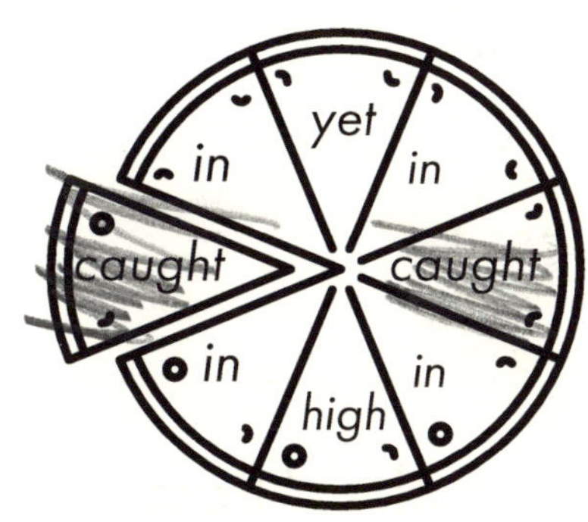

Find and circle the word "**caught**"

r	d	c	a	c	w
l	r	w	v	a	q
p	d	z	e	u	y
d	b	e	m	g	f
b	s	s	h	h	q
s	q	c	w	t	c

Fill in the missing letters to make the word "**caught**"

c_ugh_ **c____t**

ca__ht **_augh_**

c_____ **______**

We ______ a big fish on our trip.

Write your own sentence using the word **caught**:

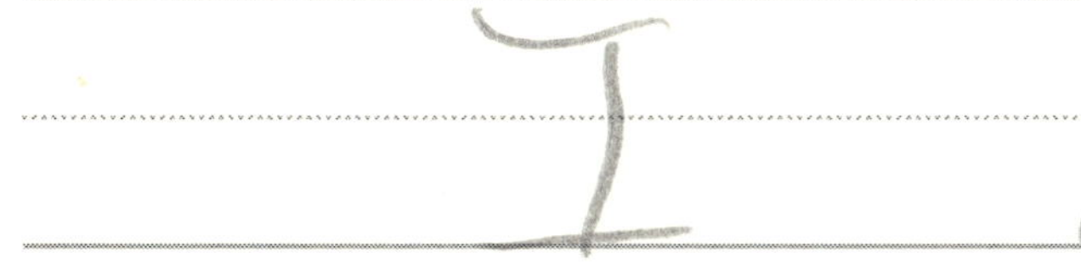

Luis is an activist in his **community.**

Trace the word:

community community

Write the word:

Color the star that has the word "**community**"

Let's work on our cutting and pasting skills. Cut out the word "**community**" from page 177 and paste it in the square box below to complete the sentence. Then read the sentence aloud!

Luis is an activist in his [ ].

Write your own sentence using the word **community**:

What **country** were you born in?

Trace the word:

country country

Write the word:

Color the pie pieces that have the word "**country**"

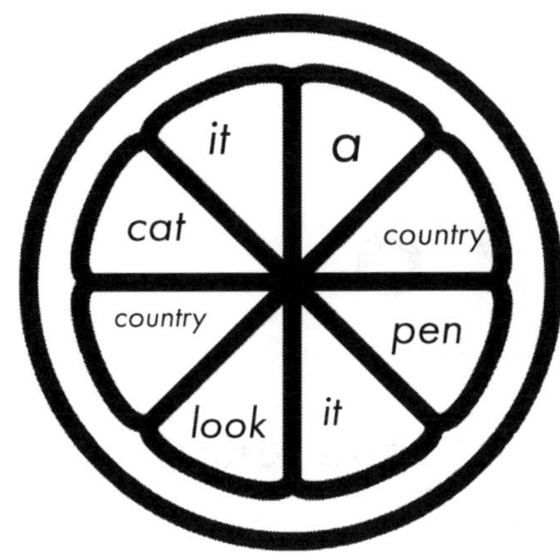

Find and circle the word "**country**"

z x a l k r t
c o u n t r y
m z e p v l q
g j s j m j n
s m k w w x c
e u p s l y m
k r r m d n f

Fill in the missing letters to make the word "**country**"

coun___ co_____

c_____y c_u_t_y

______y _______

What _ _ _ _ _ _ _ were you born in?

Write your own sentence using the word **country**:

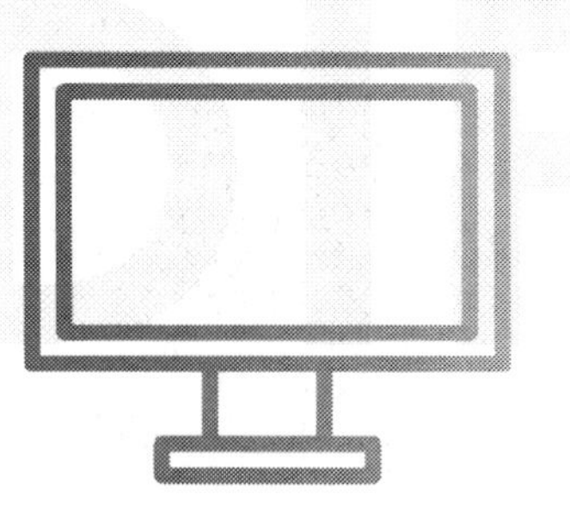

Can we watch a **different** TV show?

Trace the word:

different different

Write the word:

Color the pizza slices that have the word "**different**"

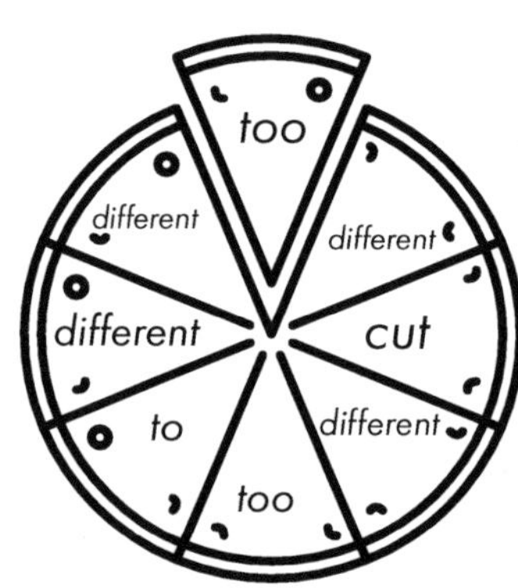

Let's work on our cutting and pasting skills. Cut out the word "**different**" from page 177 and paste it in the square box below to complete the sentence. Then read the sentence aloud!

Can we watch a [ ] TV show?

Write your own sentence using the word **different**:

We **decided** to go see a movie.

Trace the word:

decided decided

Write the word:

Color the puzzle pieces that have the word "**decided**"

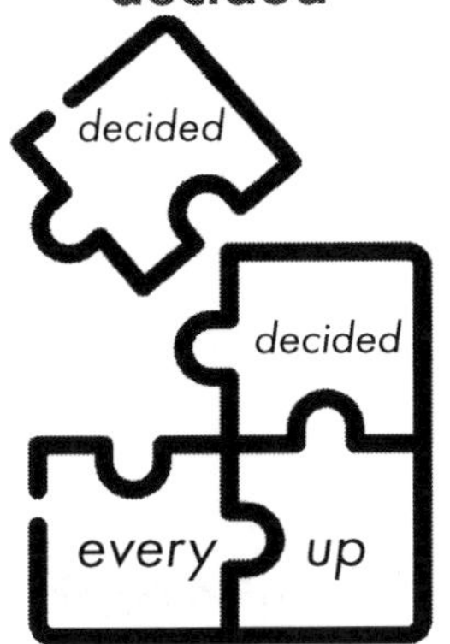

Find and circle the word "**decided**"

e	b	e	q	l	j
v	u	n	d	v	i
e	l	x	d	s	o
r	w	k	r	n	u
y	o	r	t	t	u
v	o	p	u	n	v

Fill in the missing letters to make the word "**decided**"

dec____ **______d**

de__de_ **_e___e_**

d______ **_______**

We ________ to go see a movie.

Write your own sentence using the word **decided**:

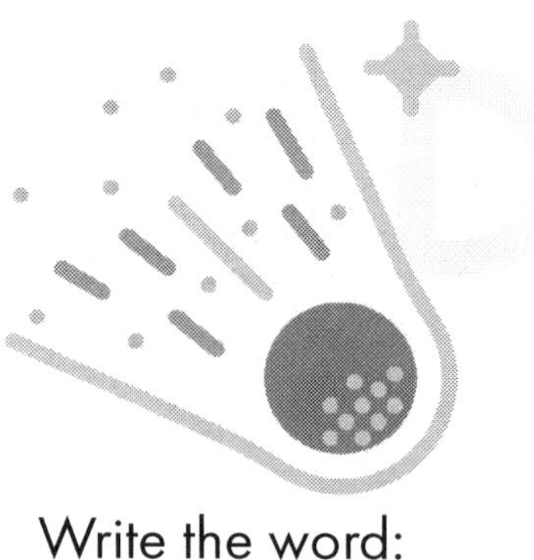

The scientist **discovered** a new comet.

Trace the word:

discovered discovered

Write the word:

Color the puzzle pieces that have the word "**discovered**"

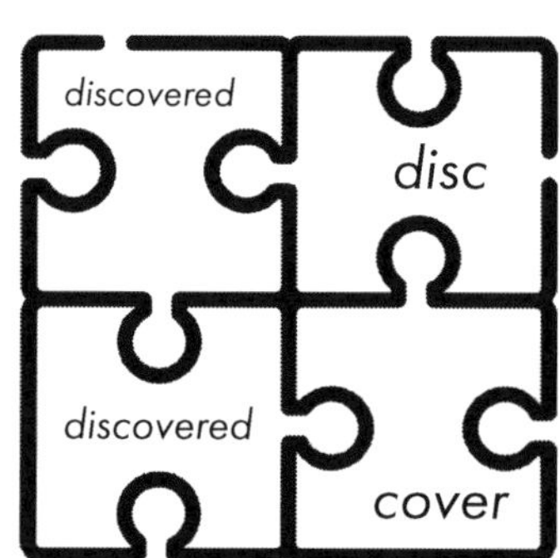

Let's work on our cutting and pasting skills. Cut out the word "**discovered**" from page 177 and paste it in the square box below to complete the sentence. Then read the sentence aloud!

The scientist [ ] a new comet.

Write your own sentence using the word **discovered**:

Does this book belong to you?

Trace the word:

does does

Write the word:

Color the pizza slices that have the word "**does**"

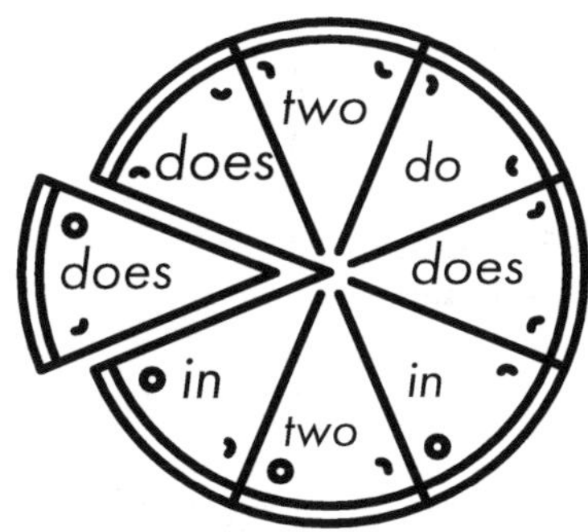

Find and circle the word "**does**"

b	g	h	p	h	m
c	z	w	r	a	t
b	g	u	f	w	h
r	j	c	o	y	z
i	a	a	j	e	l
v	v	l	c	e	l

Fill in the missing letters to make the word "**does**"

d_es do__

d__s _o_s

d___ ____

____ this book belong to you?

Write your own sentence using the word **does**:

He didn’t run fast **enough** to catch the bus.

Trace the word:

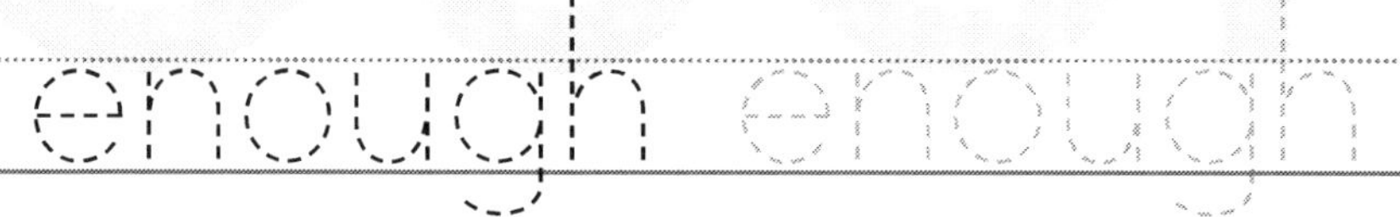

Write the word:

Color the star that has the word “**enough**”

Let’s work on our cutting and pasting skills. Cut out the word “**enough**” from page 177 and paste it in the square box below to complete the sentence. Then read the sentence aloud!

He didn’t run fast [ ] to catch the bus.

Write your own sentence using the word **enough**:

I am **almost** done eating.

Trace the word:

almost almost

Write the word:

Color the pie pieces that have the word "**almost**"

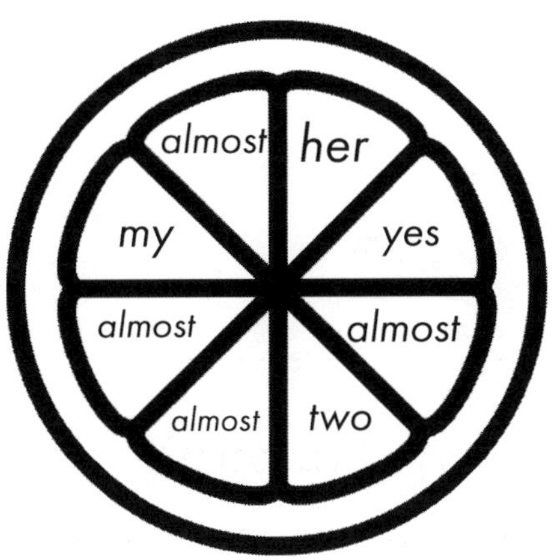

Find and circle the word "**almost**"

a	l	m	o	s	t
r	o	q	q	s	g
j	g	s	a	b	n
h	i	k	z	m	g
d	l	h	i	v	a
e	g	i	t	h	e

Fill in the missing letters to make the word "**almost**"

alm___ a_m_st

al__st a___s_

a_____ ______

I am _ _ _ _ _ _ done eating.

Write your own sentence using the word **almost**:

This book is designed **especially** for students.

Trace the word:

especially especially

Write the word:

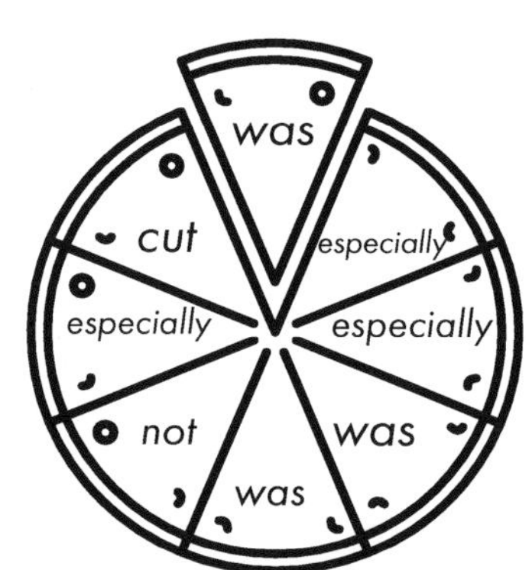

Color the pizza slices that have the word "**especially**"

Let's work on our cutting and pasting skills. Cut out the word "**especially**" from page 177 and paste it in the square box below to complete the sentence. Then read the sentence aloud!

This book was designed [ ] for students.

Write your own sentence using the word **especially**:

I love to make **everybody** happy.

Trace the word:

everybody everybody

Write the word:

Color the puzzle pieces that have the word "**everybody**"

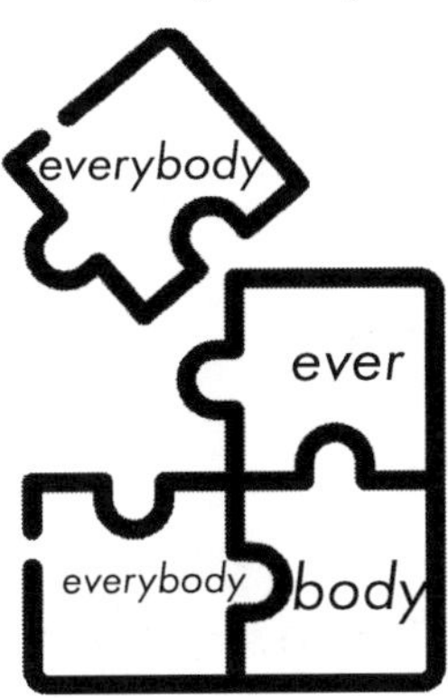

Find and circle the word "**everybody**"

e u j l g m y x n
j e s o c w d h g
a k h q x u o b t
n o g t a p b q i
h y i f a d y e y
f l j b e y r g k
d c s r z e e f f
i p v d p s v t s
y s u u m w e k w

Fill in the missing letters to make the word "**everybody**"

every_ _ _ _

e_e_y_o_y

_ _ _ _ _ _ _ _ _

I like to make _ _ _ _ _ _ _ _ _ _ happy.

Write your own sentence using the word **everybody**:

I **finally** beat Mark at chess.

Trace the word:

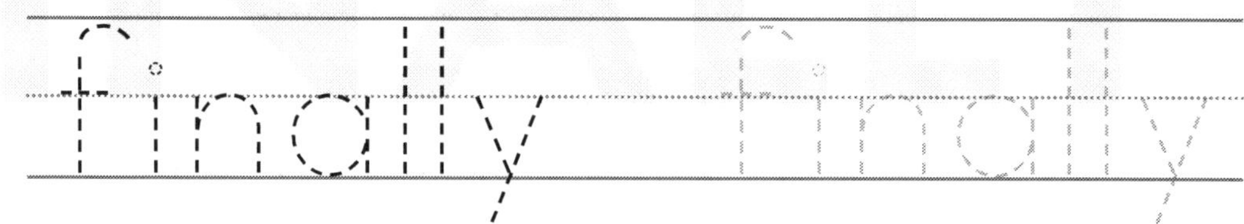

Write the word:

Color the puzzle pieces that have the word "**finally**"

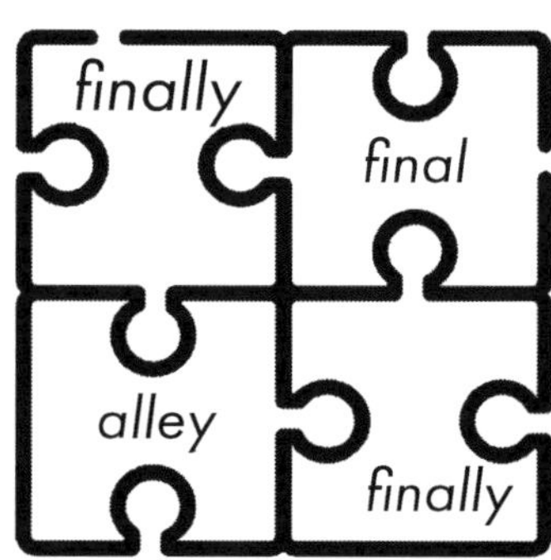

Let's work on our cutting and pasting skills. Cut out the word "**finally**" from page 177 and paste it in the square box below to complete the sentence. Then read the sentence aloud!

I [ ] beat Mark at chess.

Write your own sentence using the word **finally**:

My father works every day **except** Sunday.

Trace the word:

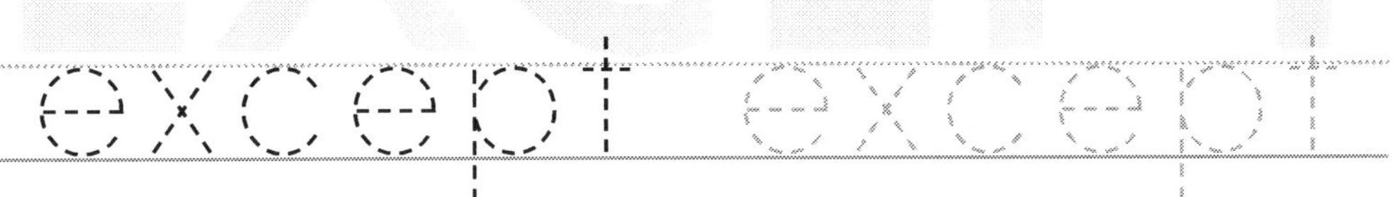

Write the word:

Color the pizza slices that have the word "**except**"

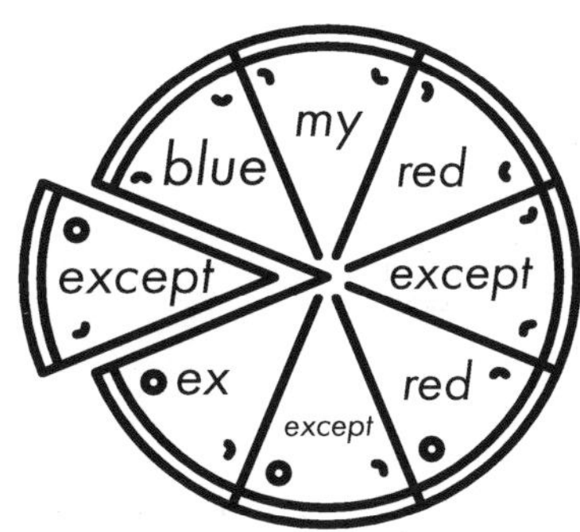

Find and circle the word "**except**"

e c b m g t
w i h z i p
f d h c z e
w d s b d c
c p f k m x
f f c m i e

Fill in the missing letters to make the word "**except**"

e_c_p_ **exc__t**

e____t **_xcep_**

e_____ **______**

My father works every day _ _ _ _ _ _ Sunday.

Write your own sentence using the word **except**:

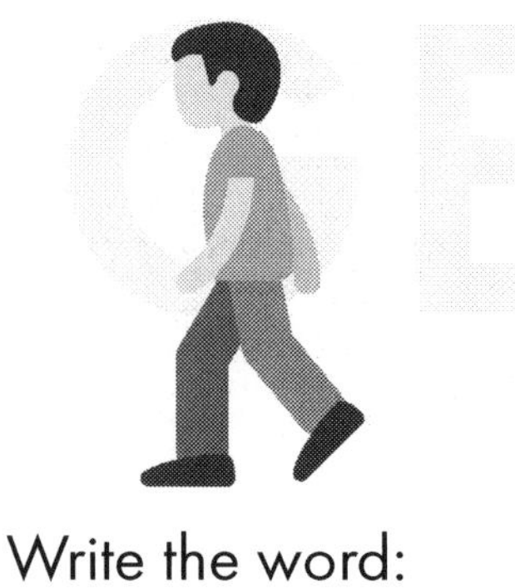

I **generally** walk to school.

Trace the word:

generally generally

Write the word:

Color the star that has the word "**generally**"

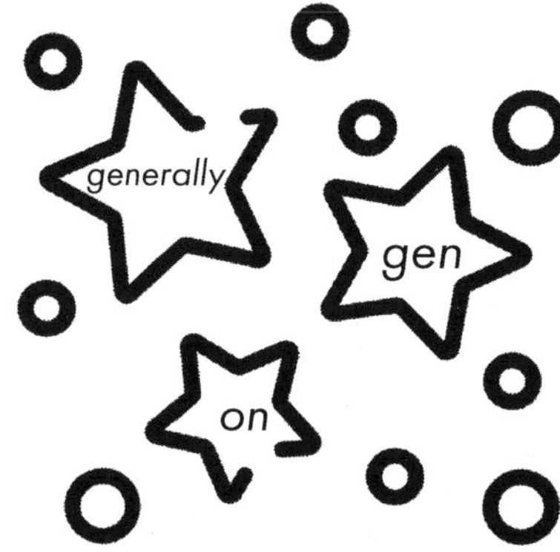

Let's work on our cutting and pasting skills. Cut out the word "**generally**" from page 177 and paste it in the square box below to complete the sentence. Then read the sentence aloud!

Write your own sentence using the word **generally**:

That cat is very **friendly!**

Trace the word:

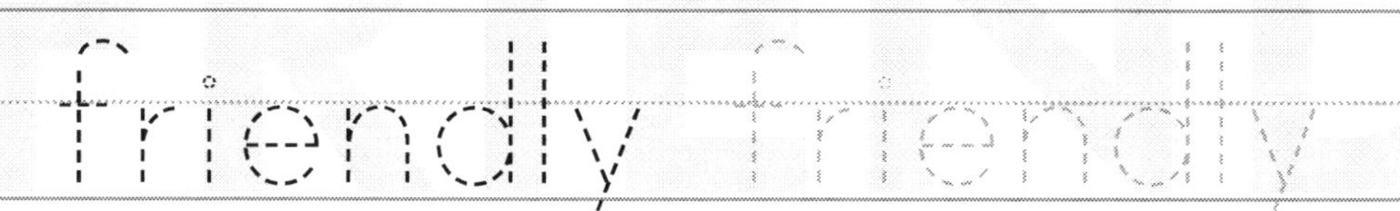

Write the word:

Color the pie pieces that have the word "**friendly**"

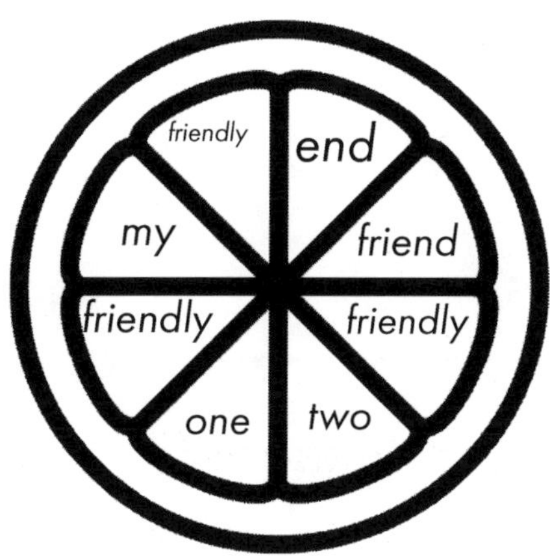

Find and circle the word "**friendly**"

e m o f x i g v
h v x n n h i c
i h i o w g a t
q i t e b g s h
v s l x u v f o
y l d n e i r f
e w q s s l r t
j m w j a a u h

Fill in the missing letters to make the word "**friendly**"

fri__dly **fr____ly**

f_i_n_l_ **friend__**

f_______ **________**

That cat is very _________.

Write your own sentence using the word **friendly**:

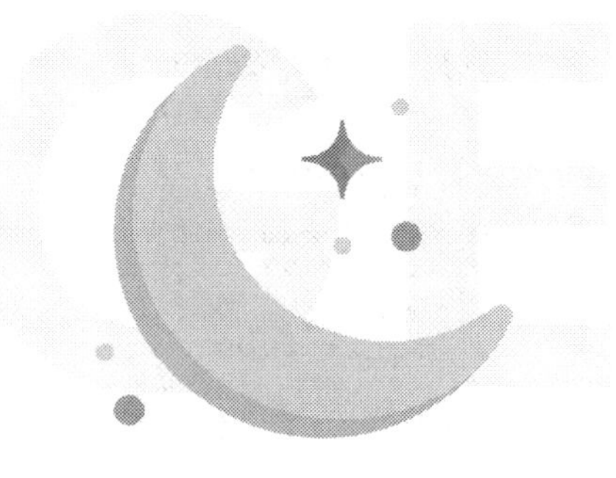

It was **getting** late.

Trace the word:

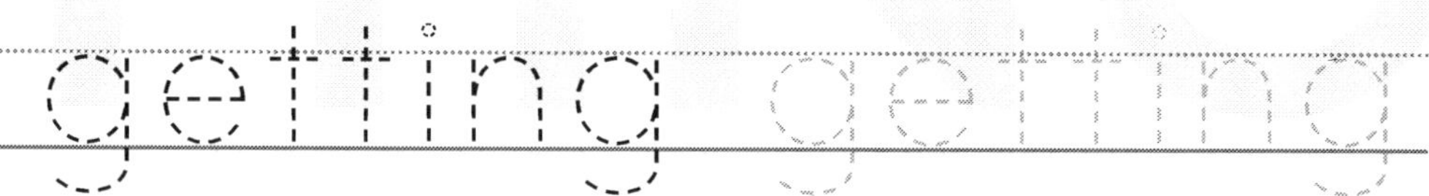

Write the word:

Color the pizza slices that have the word "**getting**"

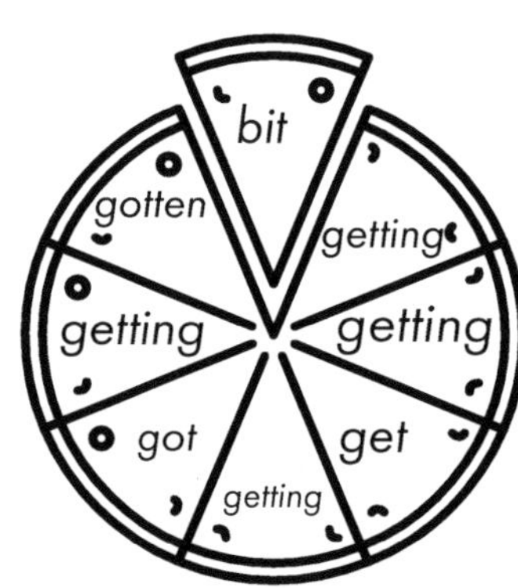

Let's work on our cutting and pasting skills. Cut out the word "**getting**" from page 177 and paste it in the square box below to complete the sentence. Then read the sentence aloud!

It was [ ] **late.**

Write your own sentence using the word **getting**:

We studied **hard** and passed the test.

Trace the word:

hard hard hard

Write the word:

Color the puzzle pieces that have the word "**hard**"

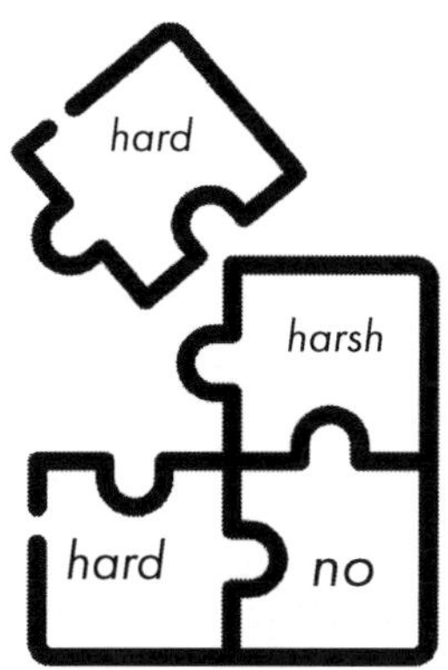

Find and circle the word "**hard**"

w	i	u	j	r	a
w	i	v	s	h	s
x	a	d	y	d	a
k	w	h	u	r	h
b	n	y	j	a	k
b	s	e	c	h	b

Fill in the missing letters to make the word "**hard**"

ha__ **h__d**

h_r_ **h___**

___d **____**

We studied _ _ _ _ and passed the test.

Write your own sentence using the word **hard**:

The moon was **hidden** behind the clouds.

Trace the word:

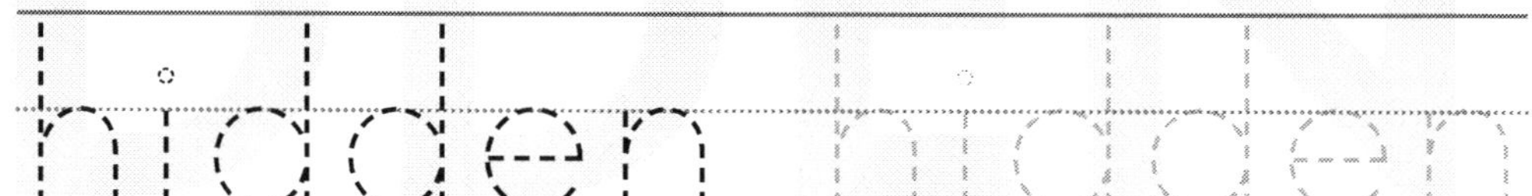

Write the word:

Color the puzzle pieces that have the word "**hidden**"

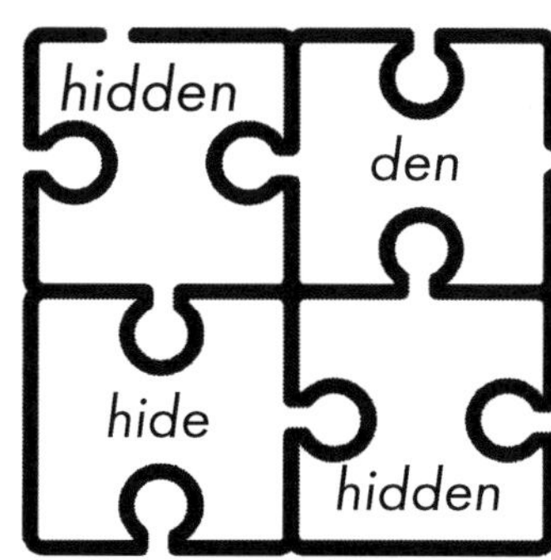

Let's work on our cutting and pasting skills. Cut out the word "**hidden**" from page 177 and paste it in the square box below to complete the sentence. Then read the sentence aloud!

The moon was [ ] behind the clouds.

Write your own sentence using the word **hidden**:

I **heard** the birds singing.

Trace the word:

heard heard

Write the word:

Color the pizza slices that have the word "**heard**"

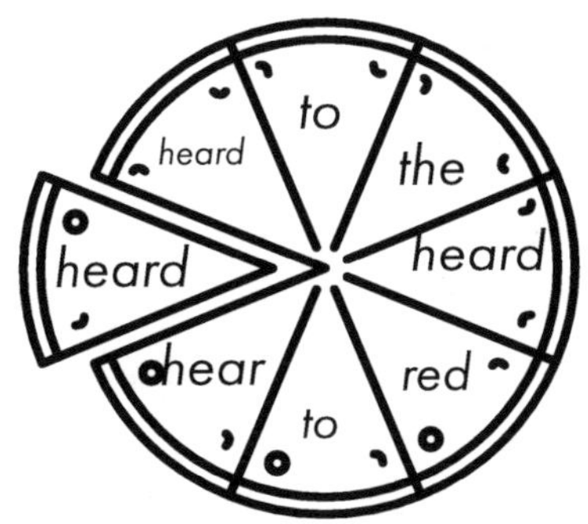

Find and circle the word "**heard**"

h	n	w	a	w	o
u	k	j	d	g	d
d	r	a	e	h	k
s	q	o	i	o	m
e	g	r	t	v	e
h	u	g	o	m	l

Fill in the missing letters to make the word "**heard**"

hea__ he___

h___d ____d

_e_r_ _____

I _ _ _ _ _ the birds singing.

Write your own sentence using the word **heard**:

This exam is very **important**.

Trace the word:

important important

Write the word:

Color the star that has the word "**important**"

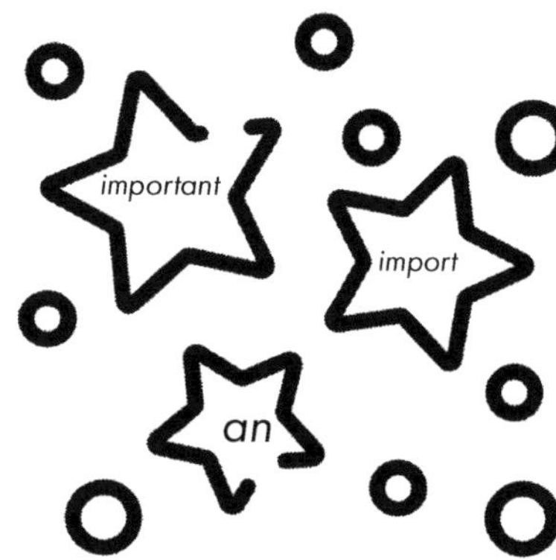

Let's work on our cutting and pasting skills. Cut out the word "**important**" from page 177 and paste it in the square box below to complete the sentence. Then read the sentence aloud!

This exam is very ______ **.**

Write your own sentence using the word **important**:

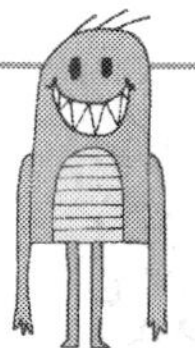

My dog dug a **hole** in the garden.

Trace the word:

hole hole hole

Write the word:

Color the pie pieces that have the word "**hole**"

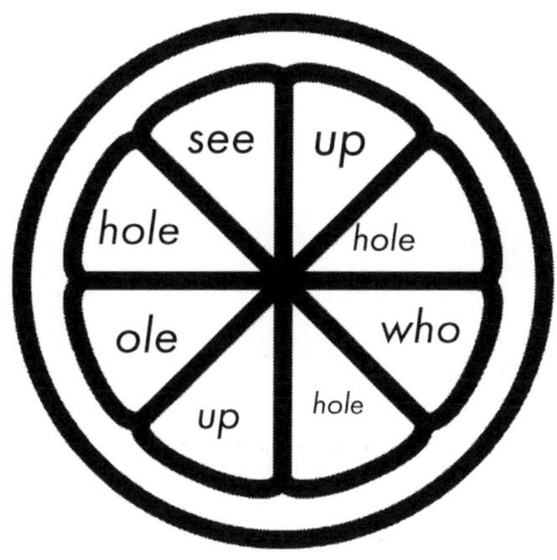

Find and circle the word "**hole**"

j s s h a t
p d o o b d
k l l l f u
e w v j r h
j j x f g c
v c n r f u

Fill in the missing letters to make the word "**hole**"

hol_ **h_l_**

_o_e **h__e**

h___ **____**

My dog dug a ____ in the garden.

Write your own sentence using the word **hole**:

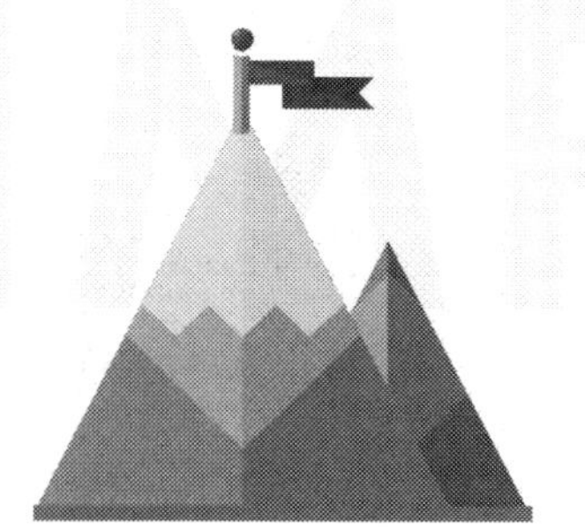

It's **impossible** to climb that mountain!

Trace the word:

impossible impossible

Write the word:

Color the pizza slices that have the word "**impossible**"

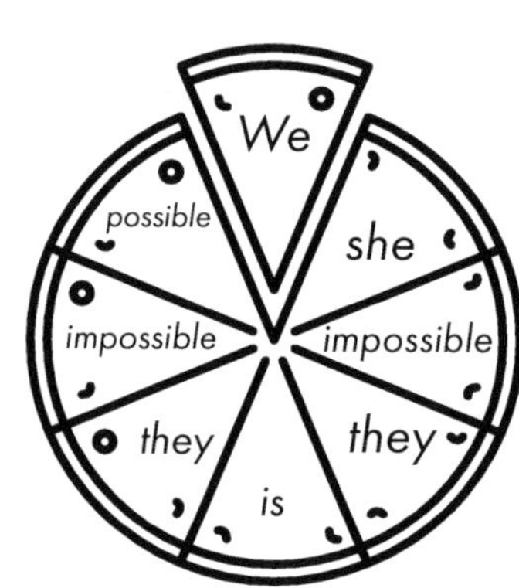

Let's work on our cutting and pasting skills. Cut out the word "**impossible**" from page 177 and paste it in the square box below to complete the sentence. Then read the sentence aloud!

It's [ ] to climb that mountian!

Write your own sentence using the word **impossible**:

Do you **recycle**?

Trace the word:

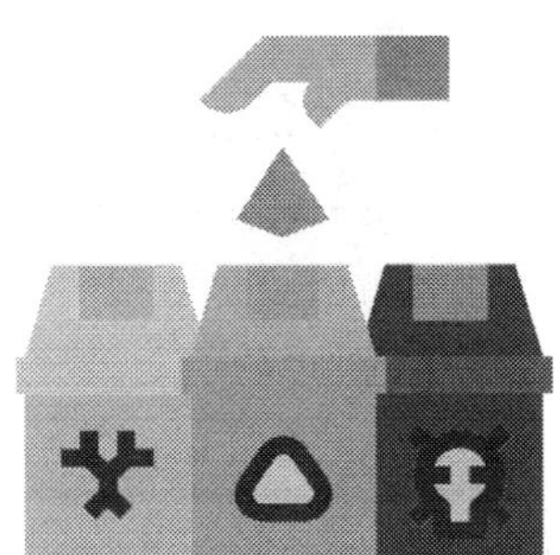

recycle recycle

Write the word:

Color the puzzle pieces that have the word "**recycle**"

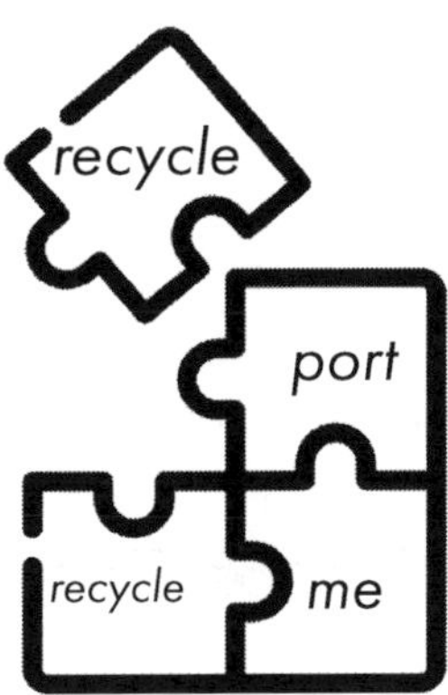

Find and circle the word "**recycle**"

w	d	n	h	d	h	e
w	i	u	w	n	l	i
k	s	g	q	c	g	g
s	e	a	y	q	q	m
y	r	c	p	v	s	i
q	e	s	g	l	n	u
r	d	l	w	w	s	

Fill in the missing letters to make the word "**recycle**"

rec____ re_____

_e_y_l_ _____le

r______ _______

Do you _ _ _ _ _ _ _ ?

Write your own sentence using the word **recycle**:

Lisa is a strong, **independent** woman.

Trace the word:

independent independent

Write the word:

Color the puzzle pieces that have the word "**independent**"

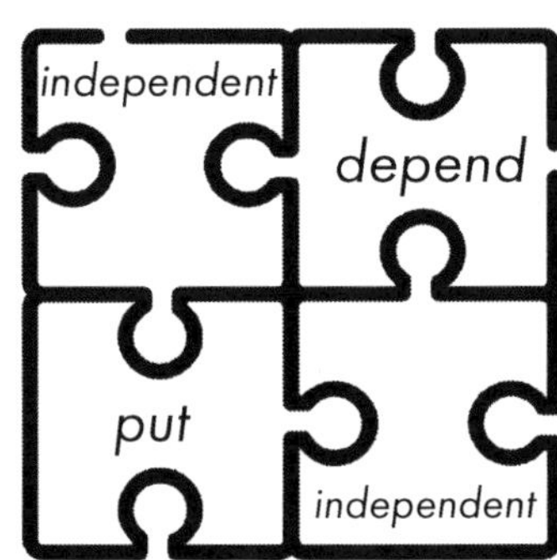

Let's work on our cutting and pasting skills. Cut out the word "**independent**" from page 177 and paste it in the square box below to complete the sentence. Then read the sentence aloud!

Lisa is a strong, [ ] woman.

Write your own sentence using the word **independent**:

The flag is on **its** pole.

Trace the word:

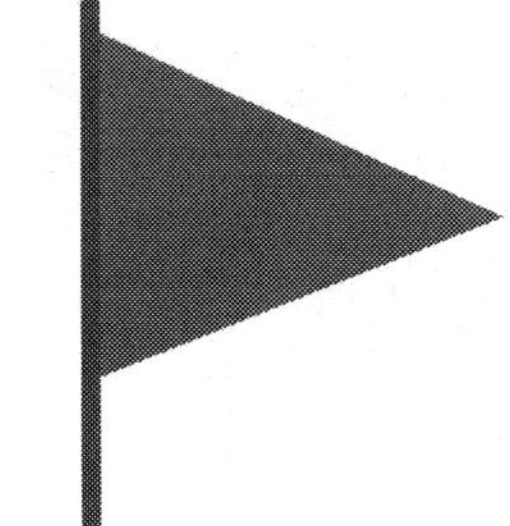

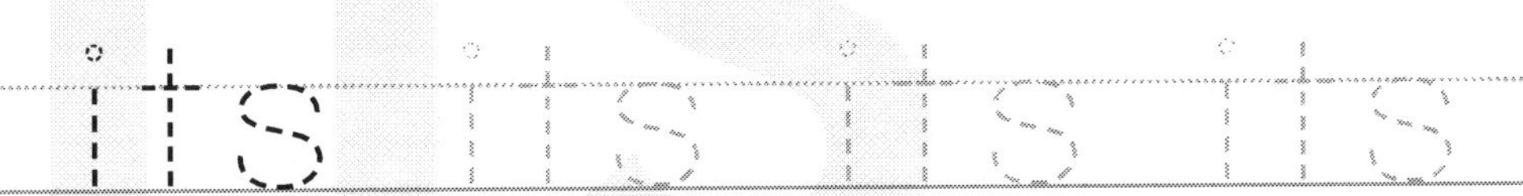

Write the word:

Color the pizza slices that have the word "**its**"

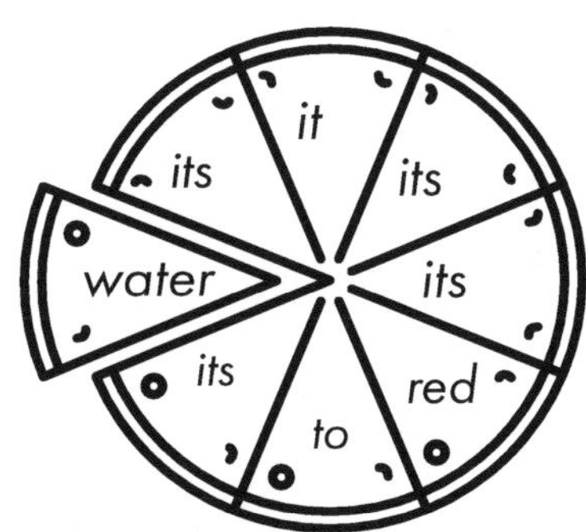

Find and circle the word "**its**"

q	e	s	v	q	r
k	t	e	q	y	b
i	z	f	k	k	c
n	y	q	x	u	b
m	z	a	h	k	t
l	d	w	o	p	g

Fill in the missing letters to make the word "**its**"

it_ i_s _t_

i__ __s ___

___ ___ ___

The flag is on _ _ _ pole.

Write your own sentence using the word **its**:

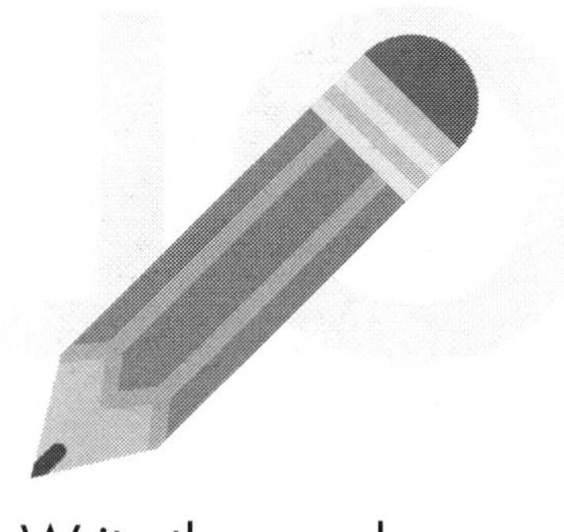

I write in my **journal** often.

Trace the word:

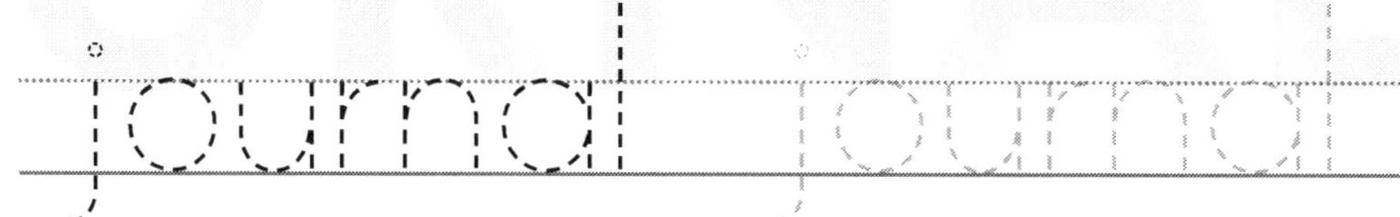

Write the word:

Color the stars that have the word "**journal**"

Let's work on our cutting and pasting skills. Cut out the word "**journal**" from page 179 and paste it in the square box below to complete the sentence. Then read the sentence aloud!

I write in my [ ] often.

Write your own sentence using the word **journal**:

He **knew** what he wanted for his birthday.

Trace the word:

knew knew knew

Write the word:

Color the pie pieces that have the word "**knew**"

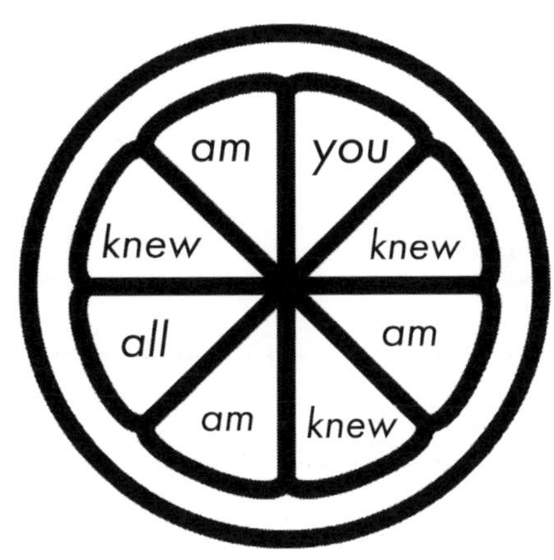

Find and circle the word "**knew**"

n	n	y	o	g	x
k	g	w	e	n	k
z	o	c	l	t	h
b	h	j	k	z	z
d	y	j	j	n	c
y	o	k	g	l	t

Fill in the missing letters to make the word "**knew**"

k__w kne_

_n_w k___

___w ____

He _ _ _ _ what he wanted for his birthday.

Write your own sentence using the word **knew**:

Everybody **laughed** a great deal.

Trace the word:

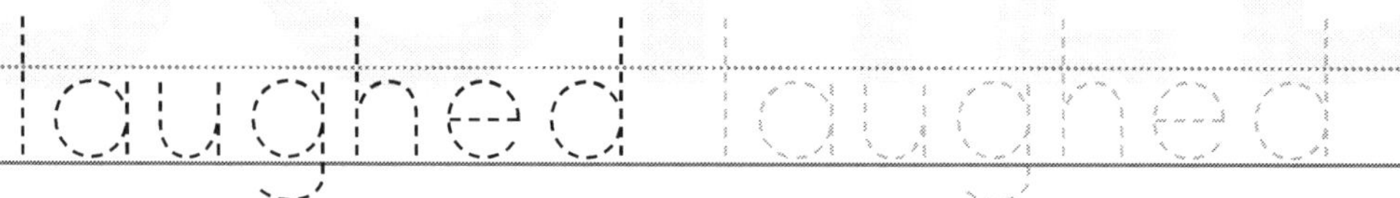

Write the word:

Color the pizza slices that have the word "**laughed**"

Let's work on our cutting and pasting skills. Cut out the word "**laughed**" from page 179 and paste it in the square box below to complete the sentence. Then read the sentence aloud!

Everybody [ ] a great deal.

Write your own sentence using the word **laughed**:

I accidently **left** my bag in school.

Trace the word:

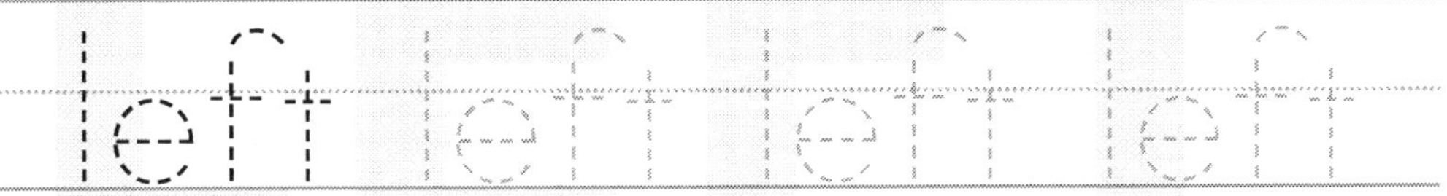

Write the word:

Color the puzzle pieces that have the word "**left**"

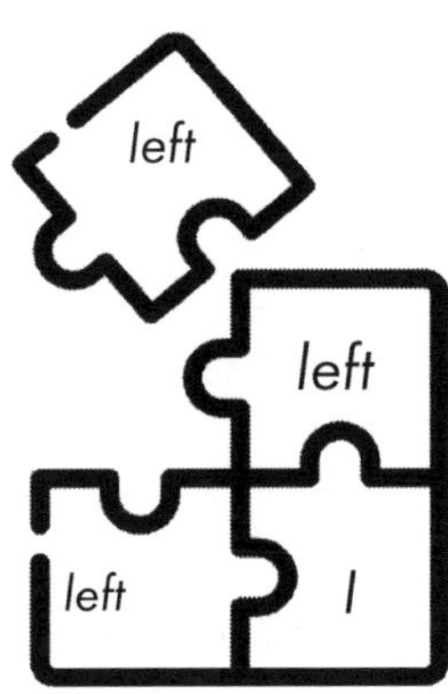

Find and circle the word "**left**"

t	j	t	u	y	a
q	f	x	q	z	x
z	a	e	d	q	j
l	p	h	l	e	q
b	u	l	d	g	p
b	i	w	m	l	i

Fill in the missing letters to make the word "**left**"

le__ l__t l_f_

l___ ___t __ft

____ ____ ____

I accidently _ _ _ _ my bag in school

Write your own sentence using the word **left**:

She is a very **lovable** person.

Trace the word:

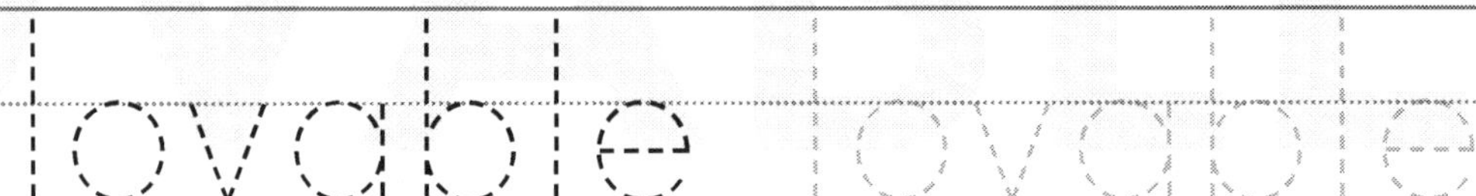

Write the word:

Color the puzzle pieces that have the word "**lovable**"

Let's work on our cutting and pasting skills. Cut out the word "**lovable**" from page 179 and paste it in the square box below to complete the sentence. Then read the sentence aloud!

She is a very [ ] person.

Write your own sentence using the word **lovable**:

I **live** in New York City.

Trace the word:

live live

Write the word:

Color the pizza slices that have the word "**live**"

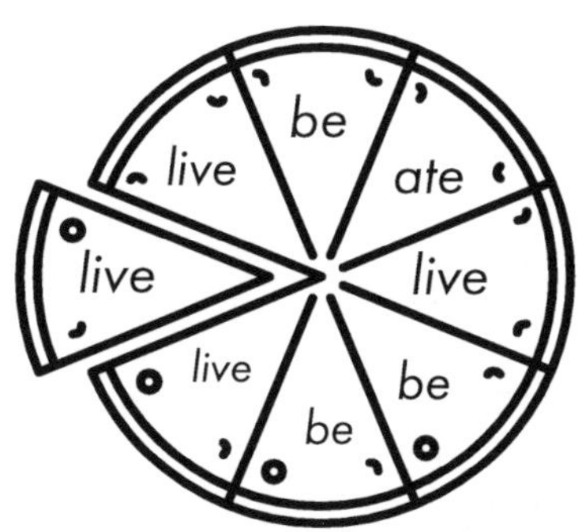

Find and circle the word "**live**"

f	k	z	a	x	y
w	j	l	d	g	j
b	r	n	f	a	p
w	e	i	e	s	c
e	v	i	l	h	f
z	h	w	l	u	o

Fill in the missing letters to make the word "**live**"

li__ l__e

__ve _i_e

___e ____

I _ _ _ _ in New York City.

Write your own sentence using the word **live**:

I take a shower in the **morning** before school.

Trace the word:

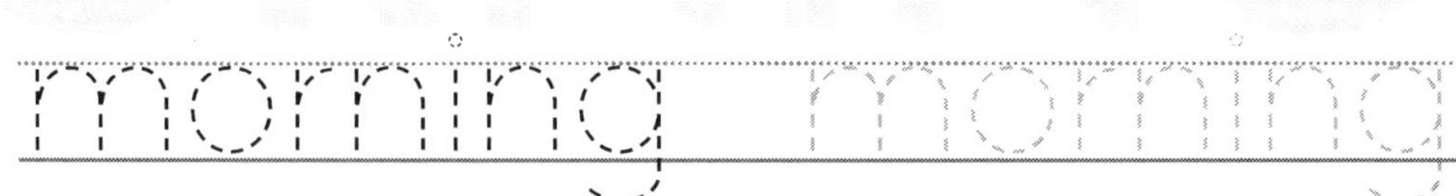

Write the word:

Color the stars that have the word "**morning**"

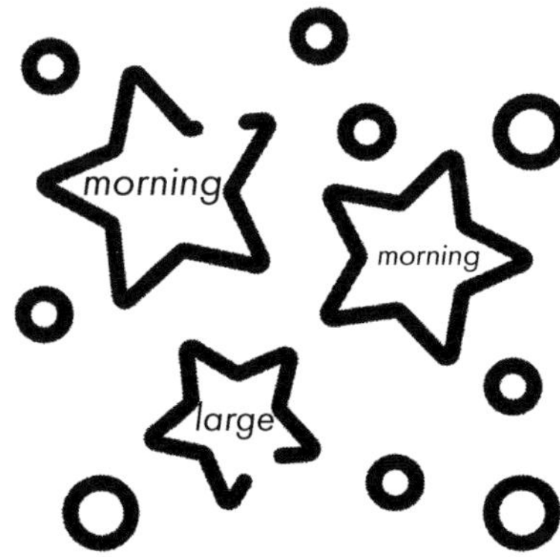

Let's work on our cutting and pasting skills. Cut out the word "**morning**" from page 179 and paste it in the square box below to complete the sentence. Then read the sentence aloud!

I take a shower in the [ ] before school.

Write your own sentence using the word **morning**:

I'm going to need some **money**.

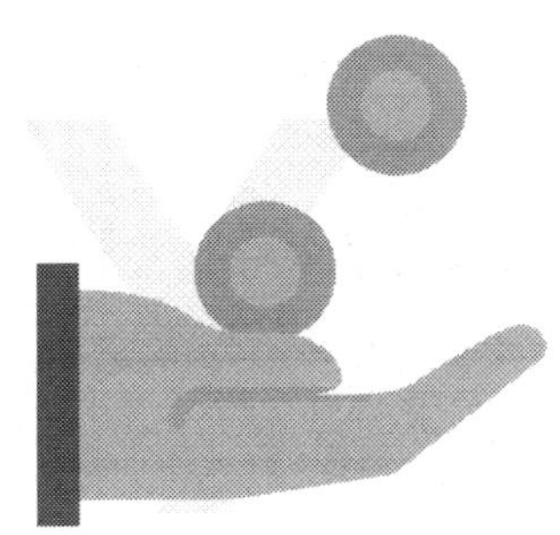

Trace the word:

Write the word:

Color the pie pieces that have the word "**money**"

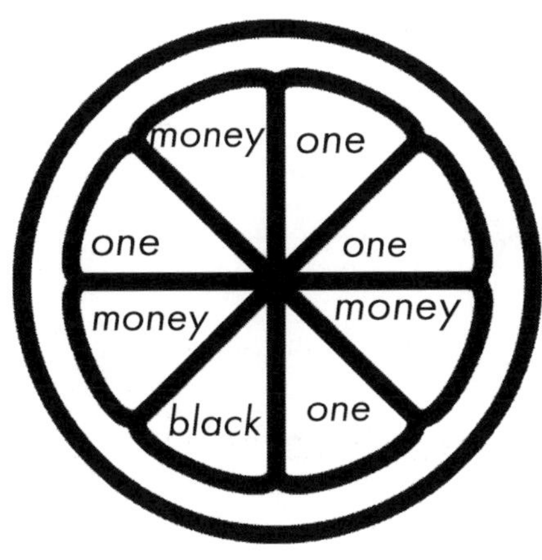

Find and circle the word "**money**"

m	n	g	r	k	i
g	o	w	m	g	c
r	k	n	q	z	e
o	l	z	e	b	l
p	n	x	t	y	f
e	u	y	j	t	z

Fill in the missing letters to make the word "**money**"

mo__y **m_n_y**

_o_e_ **m___y**

_____

I'm going to need some _ _ _ _ _ .

Write your own sentence using the word **money**:

I built this treehouse by **myself**!

Trace the word:

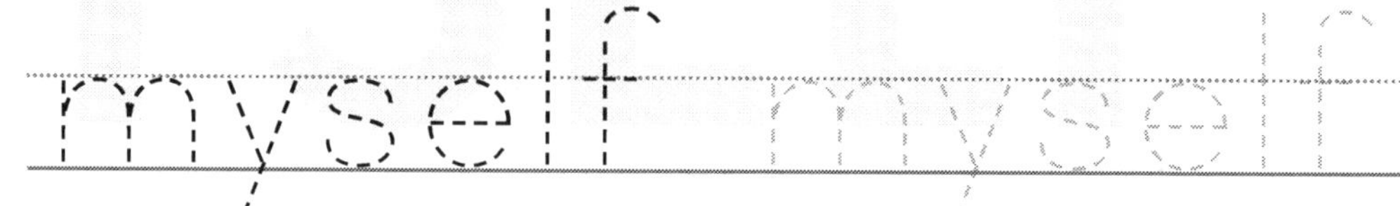

Write the word:

Color the pizza slices that have the word "**myself**"

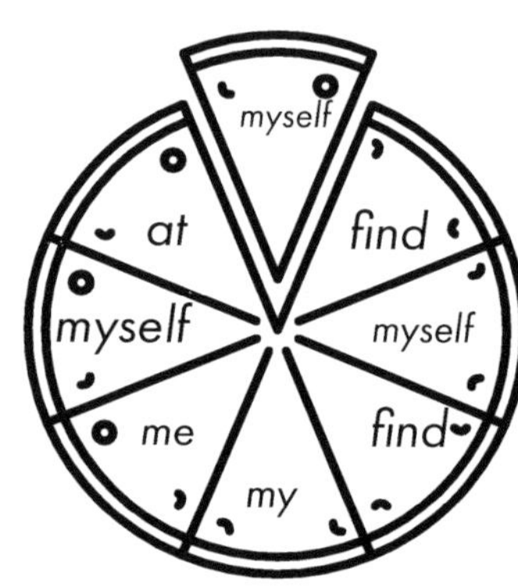

Let's work on our cutting and pasting skills. Cut out the word "**myself**" from page 179 and paste it in the square box below to complete the sentence. Then read the sentence aloud!

I build this treehouse by [ ] !

Write your own sentence using the word **myself**:

We should **never** give up on our dreams.

Trace the word:

never never

Write the word:

Color the puzzle pieces that have the word "**never**"

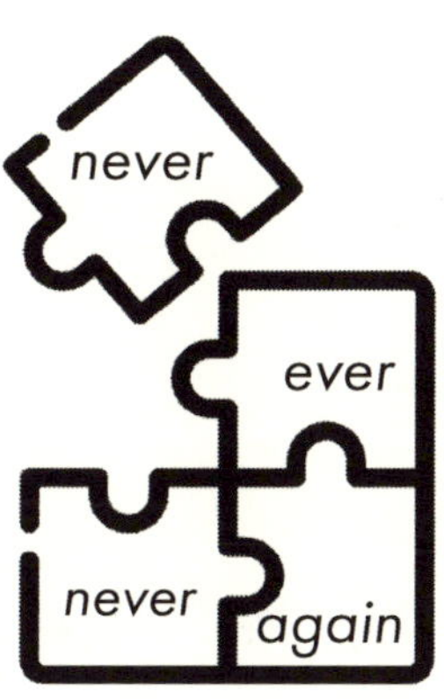

Find and circle the word "**never**"

j	i	r	f	z	n
q	k	e	k	n	a
h	u	v	j	r	g
r	v	e	e	c	b
f	w	n	y	d	d
u	g	h	t	p	w

Fill in the missing letters to make the word "**never**"

ne_er **nev__**

n_v_r **___er**

____r **_____**

We should _ _ _ _ _ give up on our dreams.

Write your own sentence using the word **never**:

How was your **night**?

Trace the word:

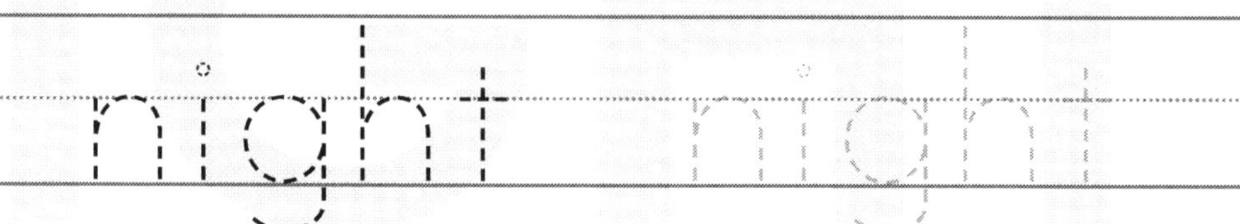

Write the word:

Color the puzzle pieces that have the word "**night**"

Let's work on our cutting and pasting skills. Cut out the word "**night**" from page 179 and paste it in the square box below to complete the sentence. Then read the sentence aloud!

How was your [ ]?

Write your own sentence using the word **night**:

Luis went to the gym **once** a week.

Trace the word:

once once once

Write the word:

Color the pizza slices that have the word "**once**"

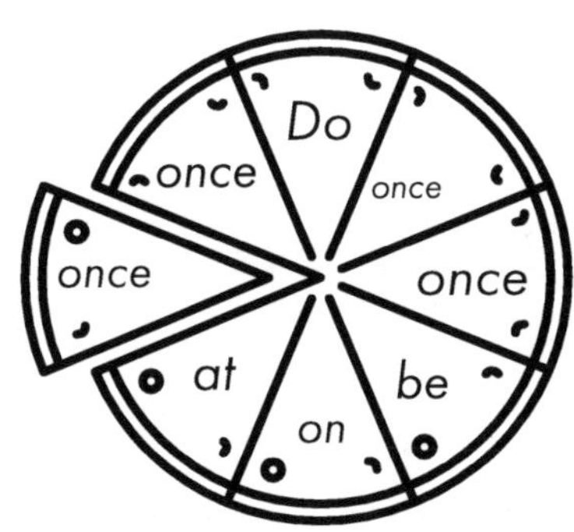

Find and circle the word "**once**"

h	e	j	i	y	v
t	h	v	g	o	e
s	f	j	s	c	d
r	h	h	n	q	u
b	w	o	s	j	d
j	z	p	u	x	i
g	x	p	w	o	s	k

Fill in the missing letters to make the word "**once**"

on__ ____ o__e

onc_ o___ ___e

o___ ____

Luis went to the gym _ _ _ _ a week.

Write your own sentence using the word **once**:

Would you like to play **outside**?

Trace the word:

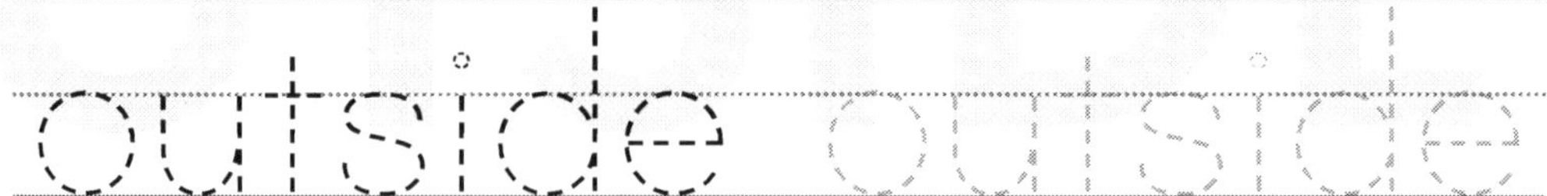

Write the word:

Color the star that has the word "**outside**"

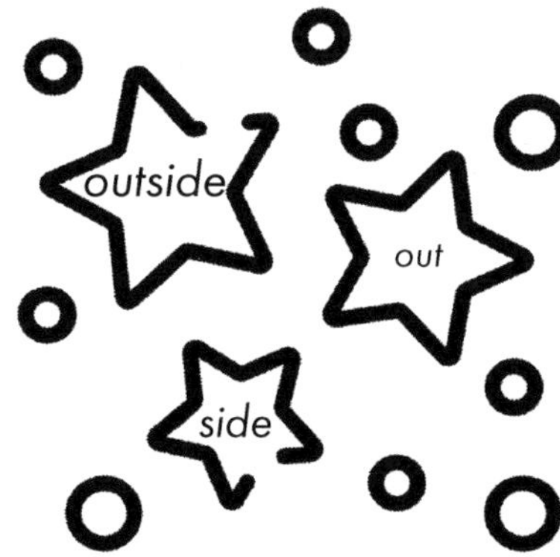

Let's work on our cutting and pasting skills. Cut out the word "**outside**" from page 179 and paste it in the square box below to complete the sentence. Then read the sentence aloud!

Would you like to play ________ ?

Write your own sentence using the word **outside**:

My parents **own** their house.

Trace the word:

own own own

Write the word:

Color the pie pieces that have the word "**own**"

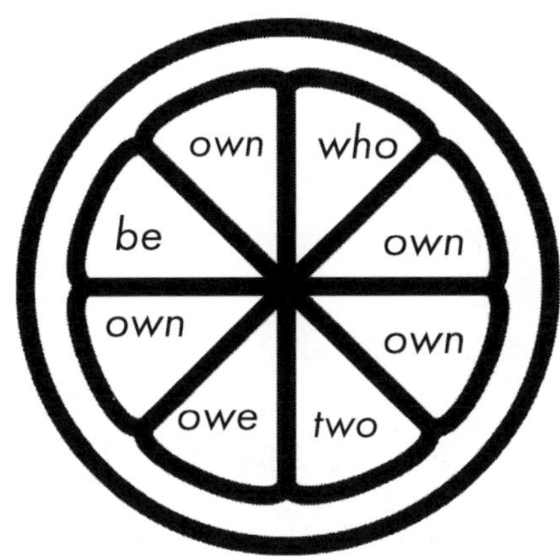

Find and circle the word "**own**"

e	w	z	i	v	o
t	a	j	m	q	w
x	n	b	h	h	n
n	t	d	a	s	j
i	s	c	e	e	m
c	p	u	c	d	w

Fill in the missing letters to make the word "**own**"

ow_ **o_n**

__n **_w_**

o__ **___**

My parents _ _ _ their house.

Write your own sentence using the word **own**:

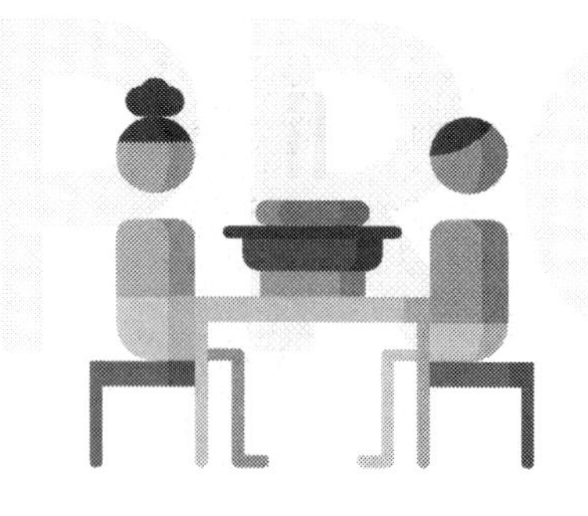

Dinner is **probably** ready by now.

Trace the word:

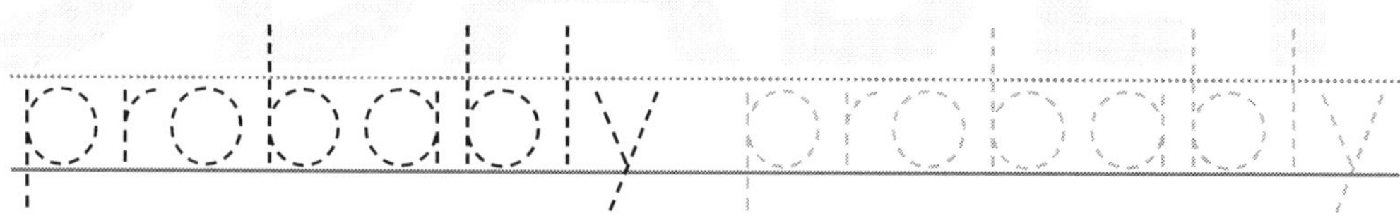

Write the word:

Color the pizza slices that have the word "**probably**"

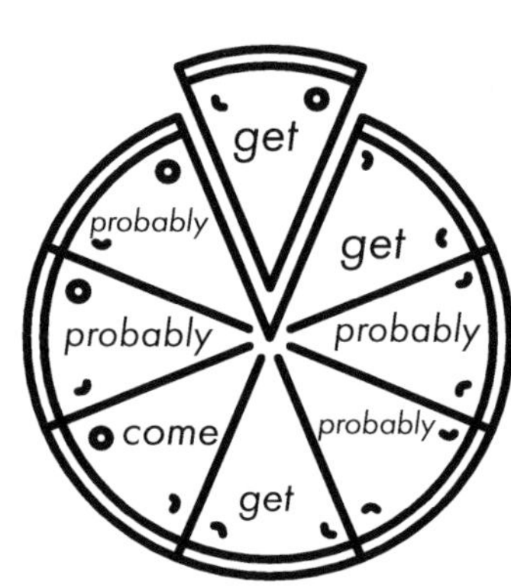

Let's work on our cutting and pasting skills. Cut out the word "**probably**" from page 179 and paste it in the square box below to complete the sentence. Then read the sentence aloud!

Dinner is [ ] ready by now.

Write your own sentence using the word **probably**:

How do you solve this **problem**?

Trace the word:

problem problem

Write the word:

Color the puzzle pieces that have the word "**problem**"

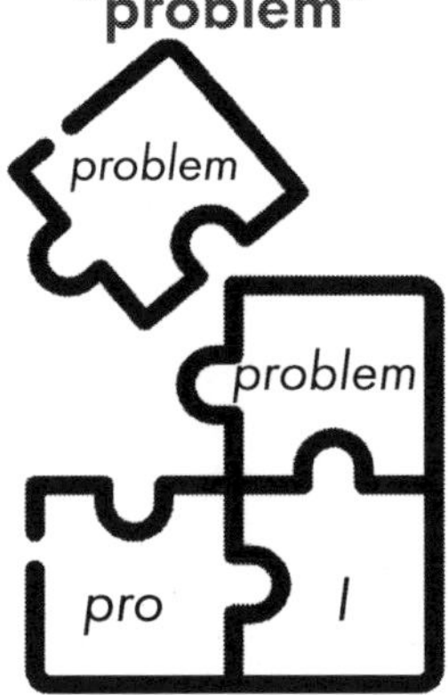

Find and circle the word "**problem**"

u	b	p	z	p	b	m
c	q	z	k	r	p	l
q	h	i	h	o	p	o
t	v	s	c	b	n	n
u	p	h	t	l	w	o
z	a	f	a	e	e	x
k	e	w	s	m	o	j

Fill in the missing letters to make the word "**problem**"

prob___ **pro___m**

pr__le_ **p_o_l_m**

p______ **_______**

How do you solve this ________?

Write your own sentence using the word **problem**:

May I ask a **question**?

Trace the word:

question question

Write the word:

Color the puzzle pieces that have the word "**question**"

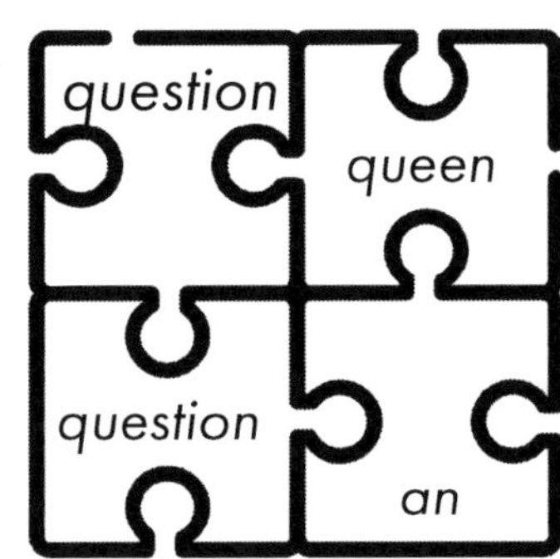

Let's work on our cutting and pasting skills. Cut out the word "**question**" from page 179 and paste it in the square box below to complete the sentence. Then read the sentence aloud!

May I ask a [ ]?

Write your own sentence using the word **question**:

Ashley is getting **ready** to leave the house.

Trace the word:

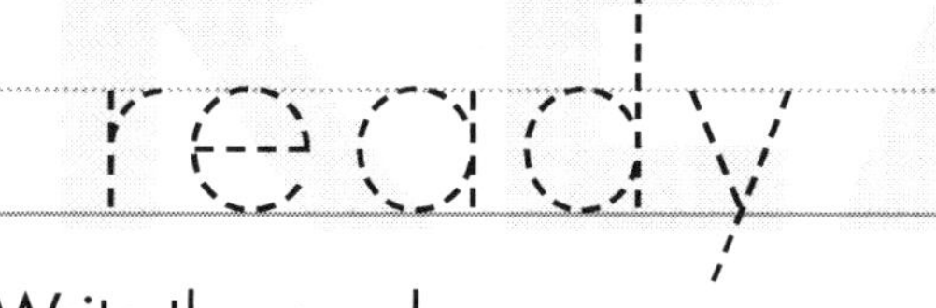

Write the word:

Color the pizza slices that have the word "**ready**"

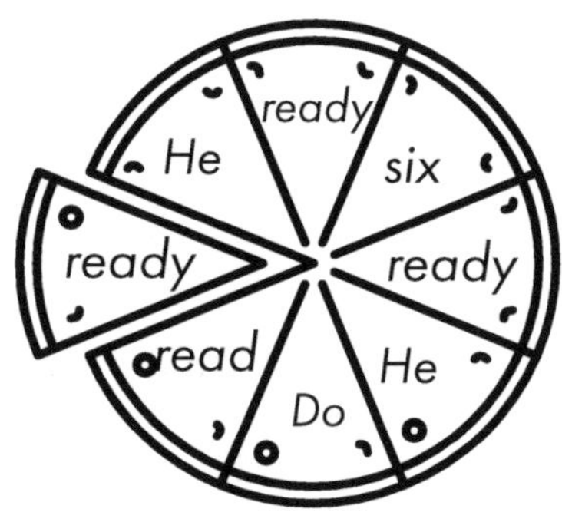

Find and circle the word "**ready**"

t	a	a	e	y	c
c	z	b	j	d	s
z	w	z	c	a	k
a	d	a	a	e	h
e	m	w	j	r	p
q	o	a	q	v	c

Fill in the missing letters to make the word "**ready**"

__ady **re___**

__a_y **r__dy**

____y **_____**

Ashley is getting _ _ _ _ _ to leave the house.

Write your own sentence using the word **ready**:

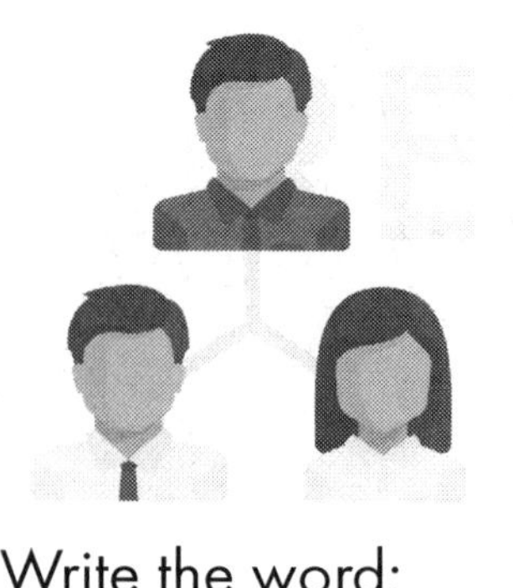

We all have important **responsibilities.**

Trace the word:

responsibilities responsibilities

Write the word:

Color the star that has the word "**responsibilities**"

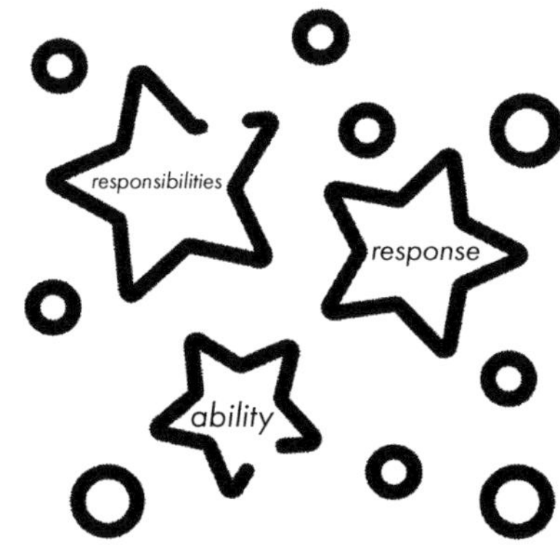

Let's work on our cutting and pasting skills. Cut out the word "**responsibilities**" from page 179 and paste it in the square box below to complete the sentence. Then read the sentence aloud!

We all have important [ ] **.**

Write your own sentence using the word **responsibilities**:

You **shouldn't** exercise on a full stomach.

Trace the word:

shouldn't shouldn't

Write the word:

Color the pie pieces that have the word "**shouldn't**"

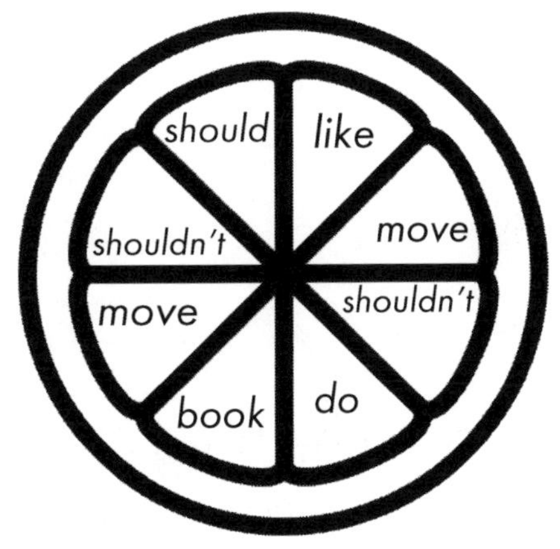

Find and circle the word "**shouldn't**"

k b d d k u e s
u e j a w p h m
r y h p x o r c
p f i r u o f v
r c f l g s r y
z w d d u v n v
z n u f l i k u
t s v h z t a x

Fill in the missing letters to make the word "**shouldn't**"

shou___'_

sho___n't

_______'_

You _ _ _ _ _ _ _ _ ' _ exercise on a full stomach.

Write your own sentence using the word **shouldn't**:

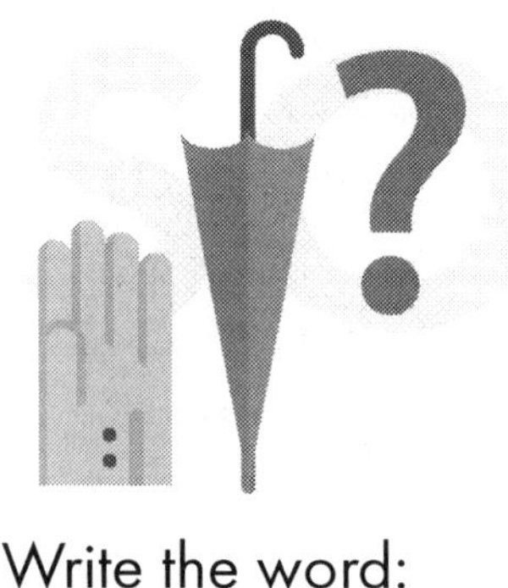

Is **something** missing from here?

Trace the word:

something something

Write the word:

Color the pizza slices that have the word "**something**"

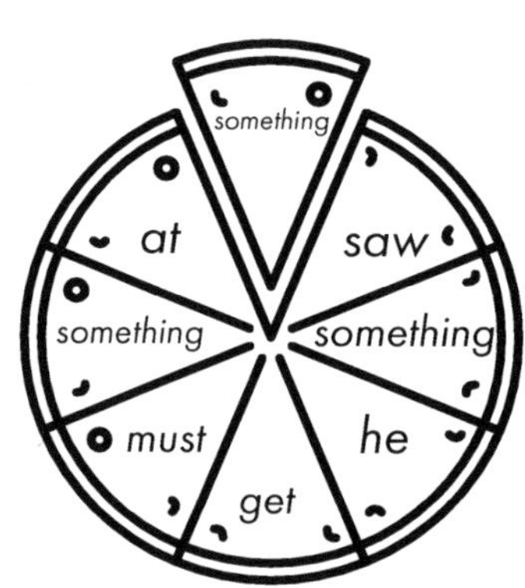

Let's work on our cutting and pasting skills. Cut out the word "**something**" from page 179 and paste it in the square box below to complete the sentence. Then read the sentence aloud!

Is [ ] missing from here?

Write your own sentence using the word **something**:

All of a **sudden**, a fire broke out!

Trace the word:

sudden sudden

Write the word:

Color the puzzle pieces that have the word "**sudden**"

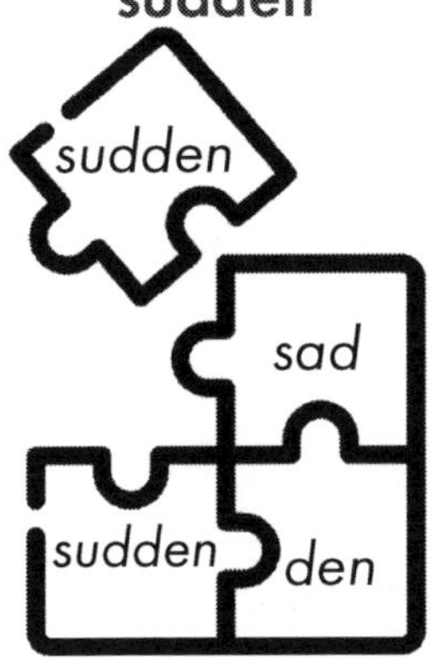

Find and circle the word "**sudden**"

s u d d e n
o t f p l j
t f g c j c
m f v n c r
x h d e y r
l w e m y z

Fill in the missing letters to make the word "**sudden**"

__dd__ **su__en**

s___en **___den**

s_____ **______**

All of a ______, a fire broke out!

Write your own sentence using the word **sudden**:

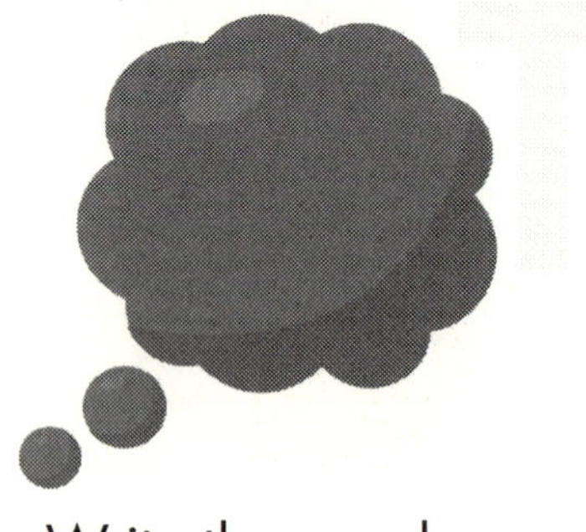

We thought the movie was **terrible**.

Trace the word:

terrible terrible terrible

Write the word:

Color the puzzle pieces that have the word "**terrible**"

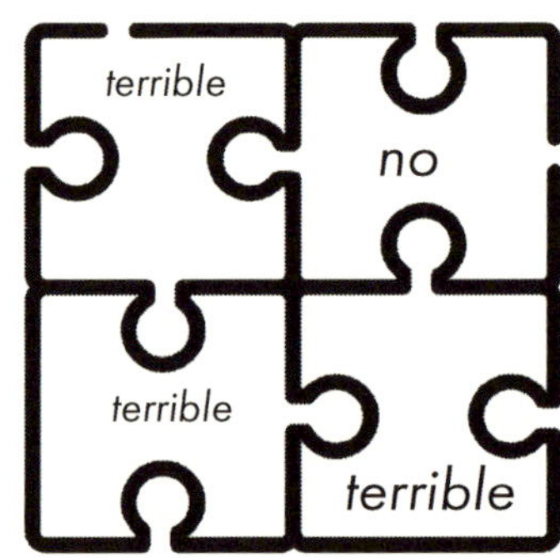

Let's work on our cutting and pasting skills. Cut out the word "**terrible**" from page 179 and paste it in the square box below to complete the sentence. Then read the sentence aloud!

We thought the movie was [ ] **.**

Write your own sentence using the word **terrible**:

Are you **sure** you want to do this?

Trace the word:

sure sure sure

Write the word:

Color the pizza slices that have the word "**sure**"

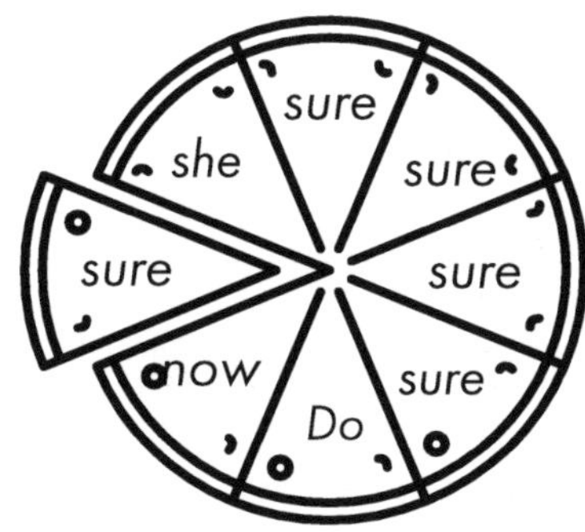

Find and circle the word "**sure**"

o q h y s e
u i o x r i
m z x u s q
w r s j x s
m f s i r u
w k z j y i

Fill in the missing letters to make the word "**sure**"

__re s_r_

su__ ___e

____ __r_

Are you _ _ _ _ you want to do this?

Write your own sentence using the word **sure**:

I hope she is not in **trouble**.

Trace the word:

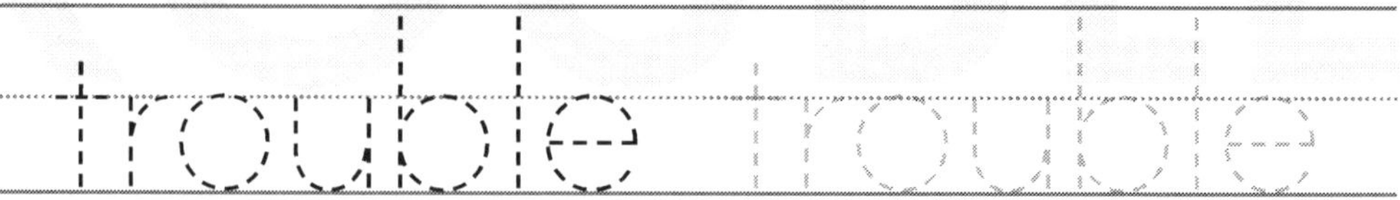

Write the word:

Color the stars that have the word "**trouble**"

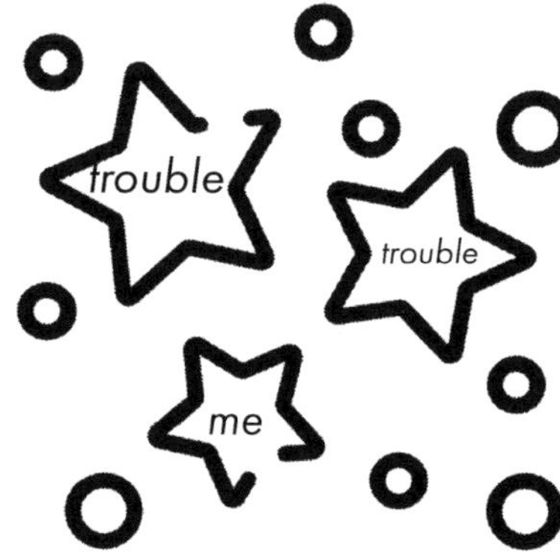

Let's work on our cutting and pasting skills. Cut out the word "**trouble**" from page 179 and paste it in the square box below to complete the sentence. Then read the sentence aloud!

I hope she is not in [ ].

Write your own sentence using the word **trouble**:

These flowers are beautiful.

Trace the word:

These These

Write the word:

Color the pie pieces that have the word "**these**"

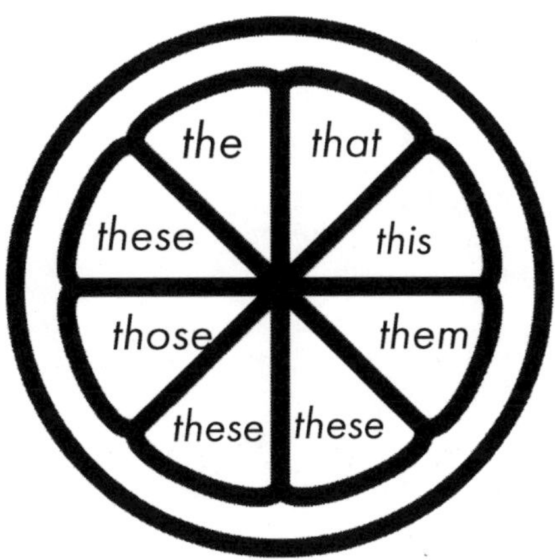

Find and circle the word "**these**"

n	r	k	e	t	u
g	b	e	s	r	d
q	r	j	e	r	r
a	l	l	h	p	u
w	c	u	t	v	a
g	u	s	u	s	n

Fill in the missing letters to make the word "**these**"

___se **t_e_e**

th___ **____e**

t____ **_____**

_ _ _ _ _ flowers are beautiful.

Write your own sentence using the word **these**:

I glanced **through** the brochure.

Trace the word:

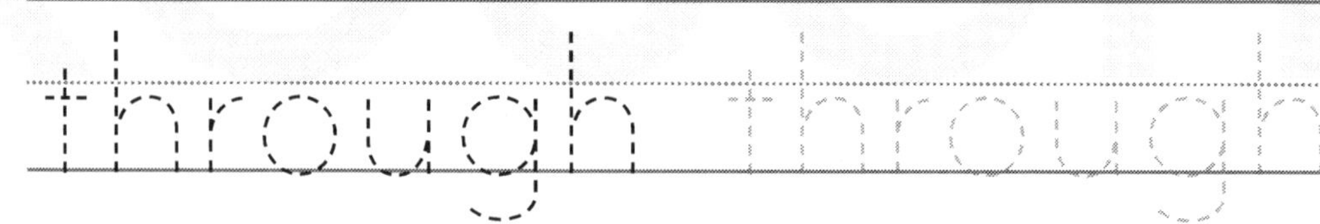

Write the word:

Color the pizza slices that have the word "**through**"

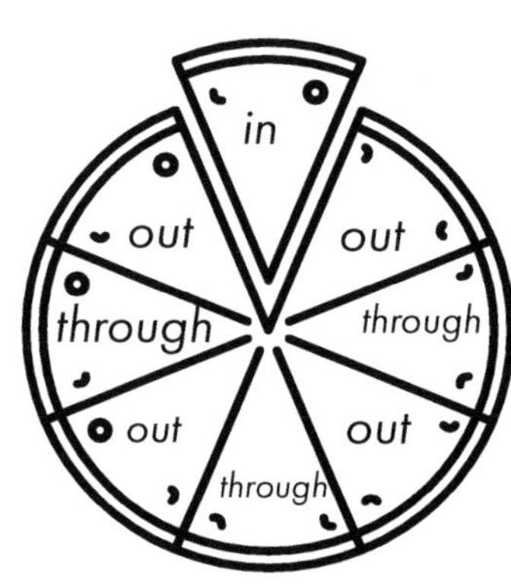

Let's work on our cutting and pasting skills. Cut out the word "**through**" from page 179 and paste it in the square box below to complete the sentence. Then read the sentence aloud!

I glanced [ ] the brochure.

Write your own sentence using the word **through**:

Jim **threw** the ball to Dave.

Trace the word:

threw threw

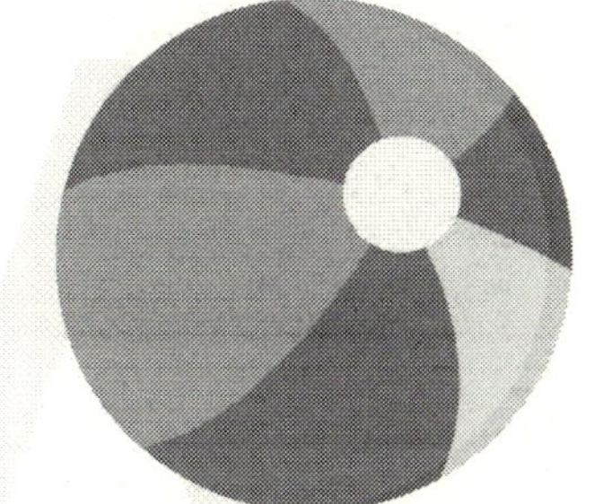

Write the word:

Color the puzzle pieces that have the word "**threw**"

Find and circle the word "**threw**"

t y q e p h
x h q q e f
v y r w u n
o d x e r y
q l c x w d
z o r b e s

Fill in the missing letters to make the word "**threw**"

_hrew t_r_w

___ew th___

_____ ____w

Jim _ _ _ _ _ the ball to Dave.

Write your own sentence using the word **threw**:

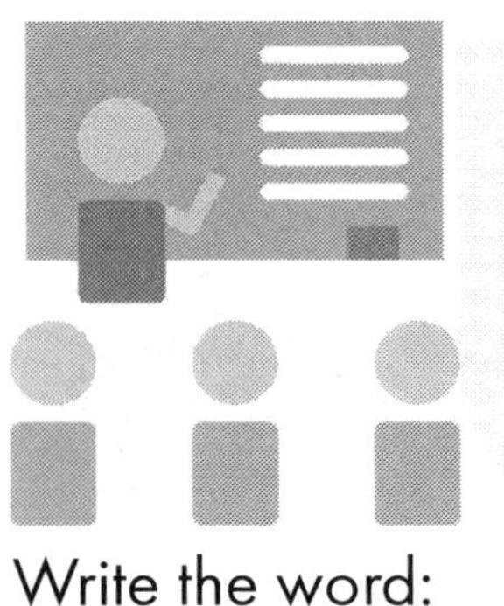

I don't have class **until** 9 o'clock.

Trace the word:

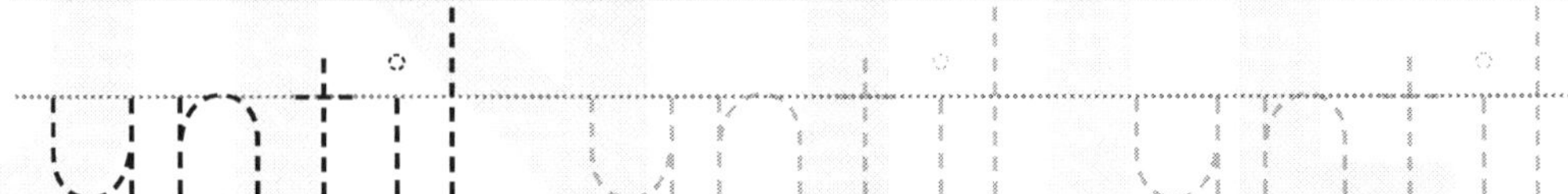

Write the word:

Color the puzzle pieces that have the word "**until**"

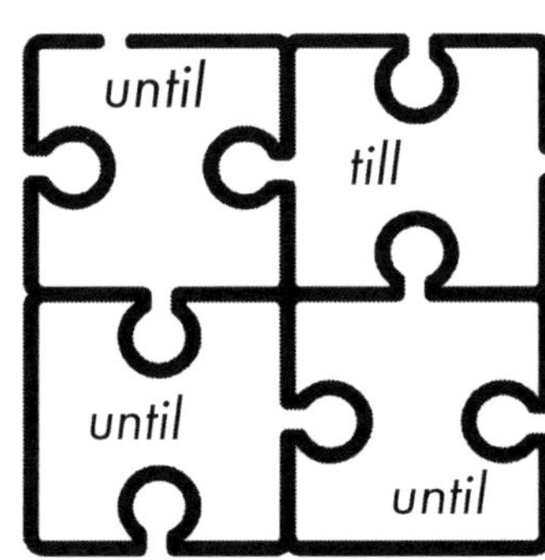

Let's work on our cutting and pasting skills. Cut out the word "**until**" from page 179 and paste it in the square box below to complete the sentence. Then read the sentence aloud!

I don't have class 

Write your own sentence using the word **until**:

My teacher **told** me I should study.

Trace the word:

told told told told

Write the word:

Color the pizza slices that have the word "**told**"

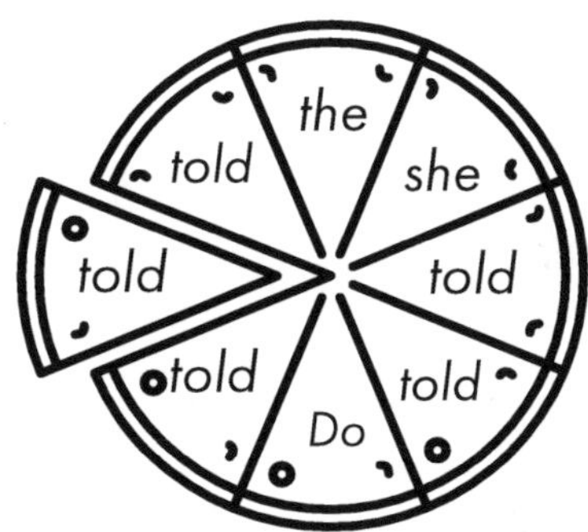

Find and circle the word "**told**"

h	x	m	s	t	o
d	b	l	g	o	t
i	m	w	w	l	j
r	v	v	j	d	j
r	l	c	n	r	p
l	k	o	s	i	g

Fill in the missing letters to make the word "**told**"

__ld **t_l_**

_o_d **t__d**

____ **t___**

My teacher _ _ _ _ me I should study.

Write your own sentence using the word **told**:

I can't wait for summer **vacation**.

Trace the word:

vacation vacation

Write the word:

Color the stars that have the word "**vacation**"

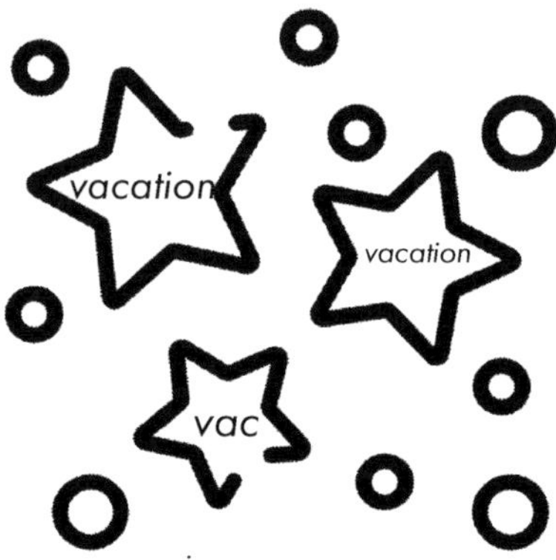

Let's work on our cutting and pasting skills. Cut out the word "**vacation**" from page 179 and paste it in the square box below to complete the sentence. Then read the sentence aloud!

I can't wait for summer [ ] .

Write your own sentence using the word **vacation**:

Please **watch** your step.

Trace the word:

watch watch

Write the word:

Color the pie pieces that have the word "**watch**"

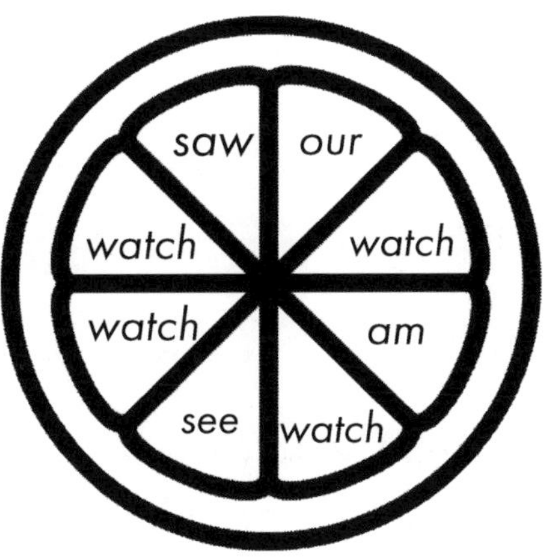

Find and circle the word "**watch**"

o	e	i	k	s	k
v	n	n	n	b	g
g	h	q	q	j	x
g	i	q	b	b	h
f	j	v	b	z	m
u	n	j	e	e	k

Fill in the missing letters to make the word "**watch**"

_ _ _ch wa_ _h

_a_c_ w_ _ _h

_ _ _ _ _ w_ _ _ _

Please _ _ _ _ _ your step.

Write your own sentence using the word **watch**:

The **weather** is looking great all week!

Trace the word:

weather weather

Write the word:

Color the pizza slices that have the word "**weather**"

Let's work on our cutting and pasting skills. Cut out the word "**weather**" from page 179 and paste it in the square box below to complete the sentence. Then read the sentence aloud!

The [ ] is looking great all week!

Write your own sentence using the word **weather**:

What are you going to **wear** to the party?

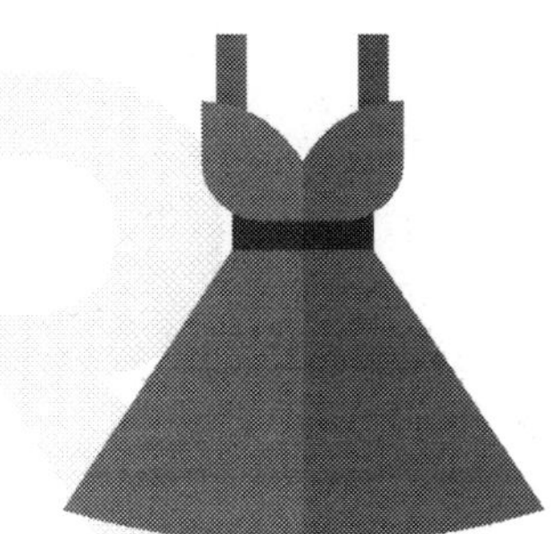

Trace the word:

wear wear wear

Write the word:

Color the puzzle pieces that have the word "**wear**"

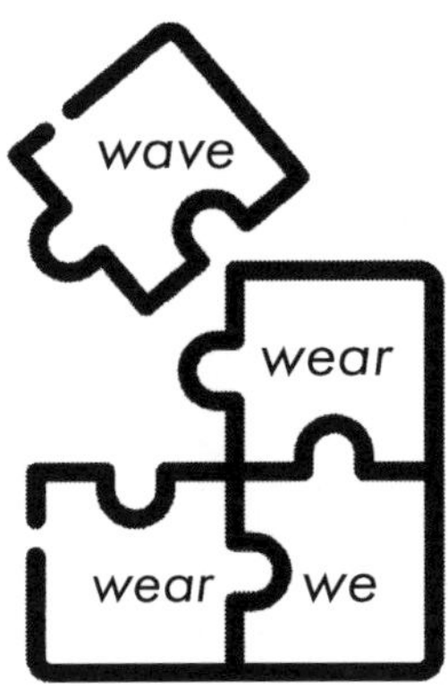

Find and circle the word "**wear**"

w	f	n	t	w	l
r	e	z	j	n	t
z	s	a	w	c	f
k	m	d	r	o	e
g	w	l	n	l	c
u	w	k	e	r	a

Fill in the missing letters to make the word "**wear**"

_ear **we__**

_e_r **w__r**

____

What are you going to ____ to the party?

Write your own sentence using the word **wear**:

Which subject do you like best?

Trace the word:

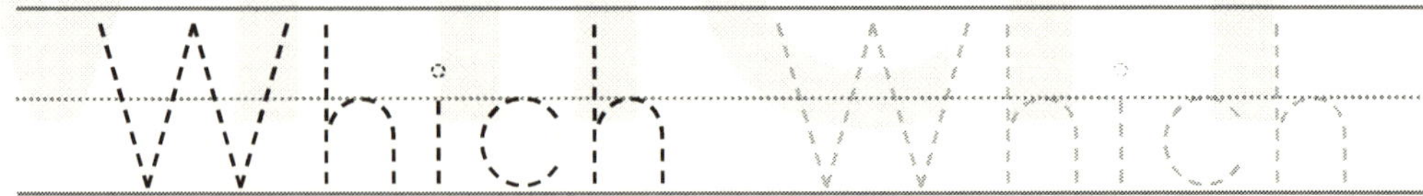

Write the word:

Color the puzzle pieces that have the word "**which**"

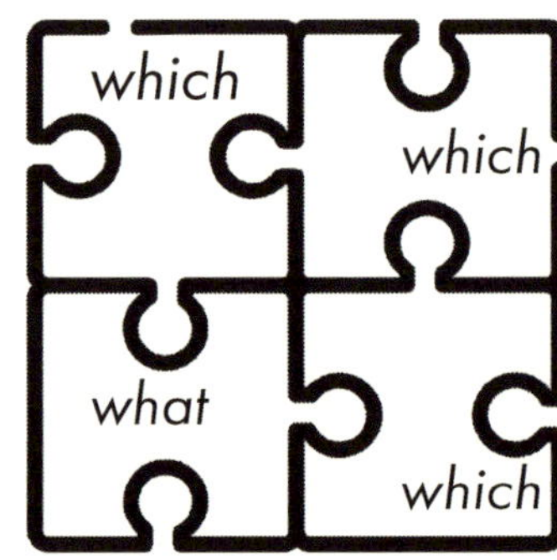

Let's work on our cutting and pasting skills. Cut out the word "**which**" from page 179 and paste it in the square box below to complete the sentence. Then read the sentence aloud!

subject do you like best ?

Write your own sentence using the word **which**:

I fell asleep **while** reading a book.

Trace the word:

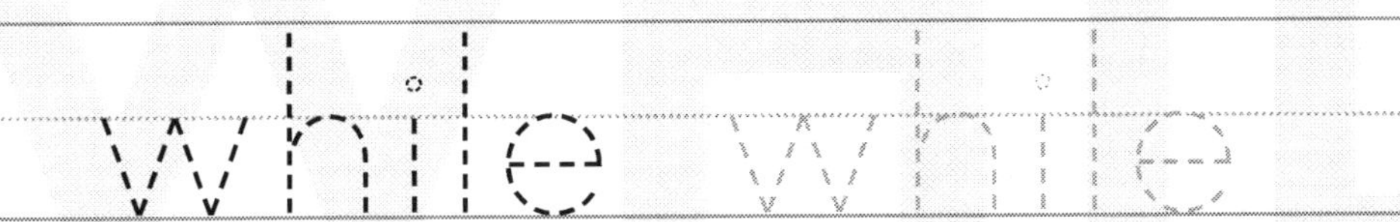

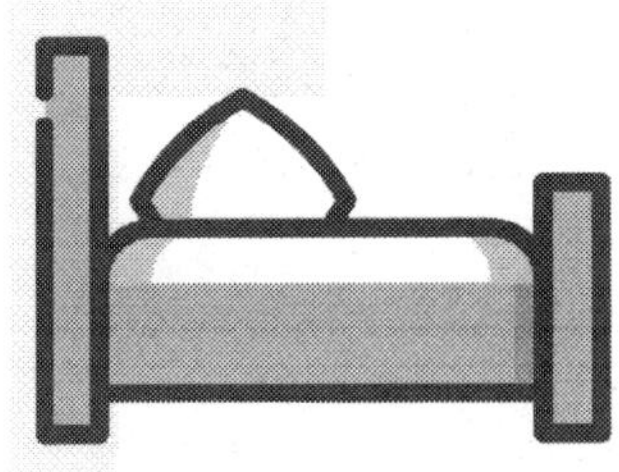

Write the word:

Color the pizza slices that have the word "**while**"

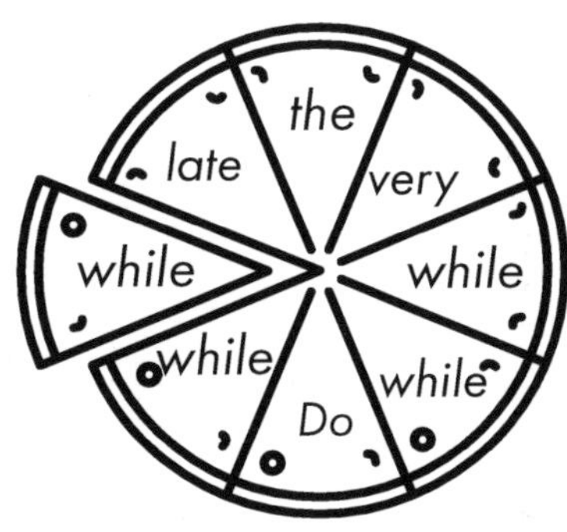

Find and circle the word "**while**"

i	e	c	i	m	k
m	l	w	g	e	a
q	i	q	x	m	s
l	h	r	t	h	u
t	w	l	r	o	y
l	g	h	i	t	a

Fill in the missing letters to make the word "**while**"

___le **wh___**

w___e **__il_**

w____ **_____**

I fell asleep _ _ _ _ _ reading a book.

Write your own sentence using the word **while**:

We spent the **whole** day fishing.

Trace the word:

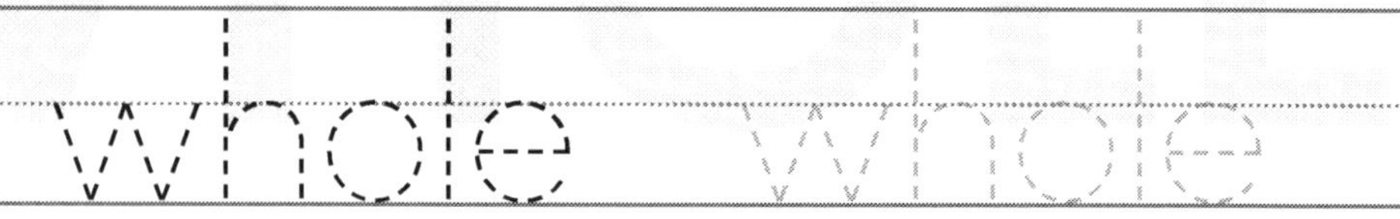

Write the word:

Color the stars that have the word "**whole**"

Let's work on our cutting and pasting skills. Cut out the word "**whole**" from page 179 and paste it in the square box below to complete the sentence. Then read the sentence aloud!

We spent the [   ] day fishing.

Write your own sentence using the word **whole**:

We went to China last **year**.

Trace the word:

year year year

Write the word:

Color the pie pieces that have the word "**year**"

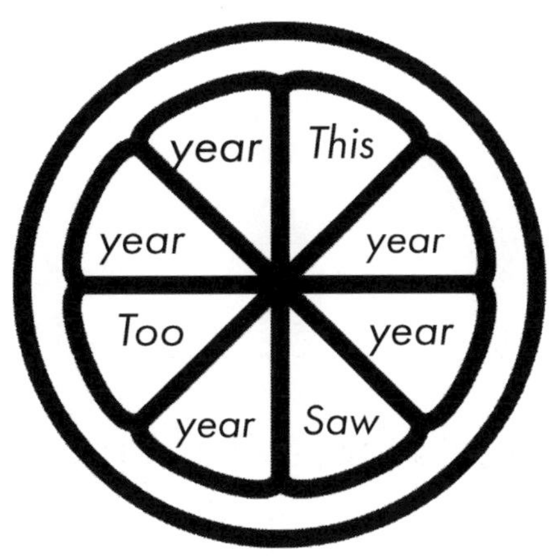

Find and circle the word "**year**"

s	t	i	r	q	v
u	m	u	u	f	n
u	n	a	o	c	c
r	u	q	f	m	x
c	t	h	h	t	q
g	r	y	g	x	p

Fill in the missing letters to make the word "**year**"

_ear y_a_

__ar y__r

y___ ____

We went to China last _ _ _ _ .

Write your own sentence using the word **year**:

Are you sure **you're** alright?

Trace the word:

you're you're

Write the word:

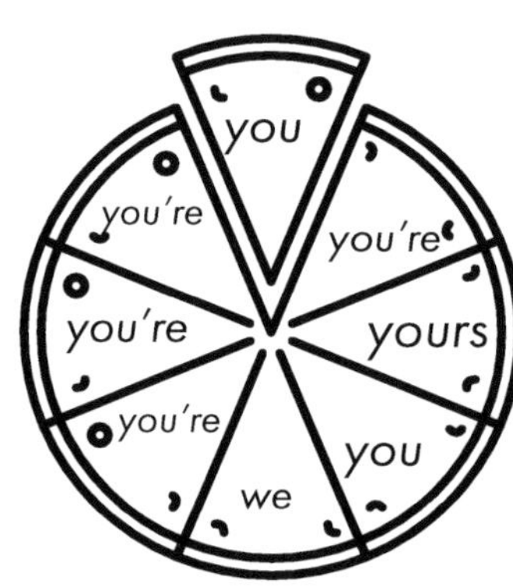

Color the pizza slices that have the word "**you're**"

Let's work on our cutting and pasting skills. Cut out the word "**you're**" from page 179 and paste it in the square box below to complete the sentence. Then read the sentence aloud!

Are you sure [ ] alright?

Write your own sentence using the word **you're**:

May I borrow **your** book?

Trace the word:

your your your

Write the word:

Color the puzzle pieces that have the word "**your**"

Find and circle the word "**your**"

b	q	v	w	k	i
u	c	m	x	v	v
w	i	l	s	r	n
a	p	i	u	u	q
p	h	g	f	b	h
t	q	z	l	k	u

Fill in the missing letters to make the word "**your**"

you_ _our yo__

___r _o__ ____

____ ____ ____

May I borrow ____ book?

Write your own sentence using the word **your**:

Sight Words you need to know

CUT & PASTE

Instructions:

Locate the correct sight words and cut out the words carefully! Paste the sight words into the corresponding pages.

BRAIN
HUNTER

Instructions:
Locate the correct sight words and cut out the words carefully!
Paste the sight words into the corresponding pages.

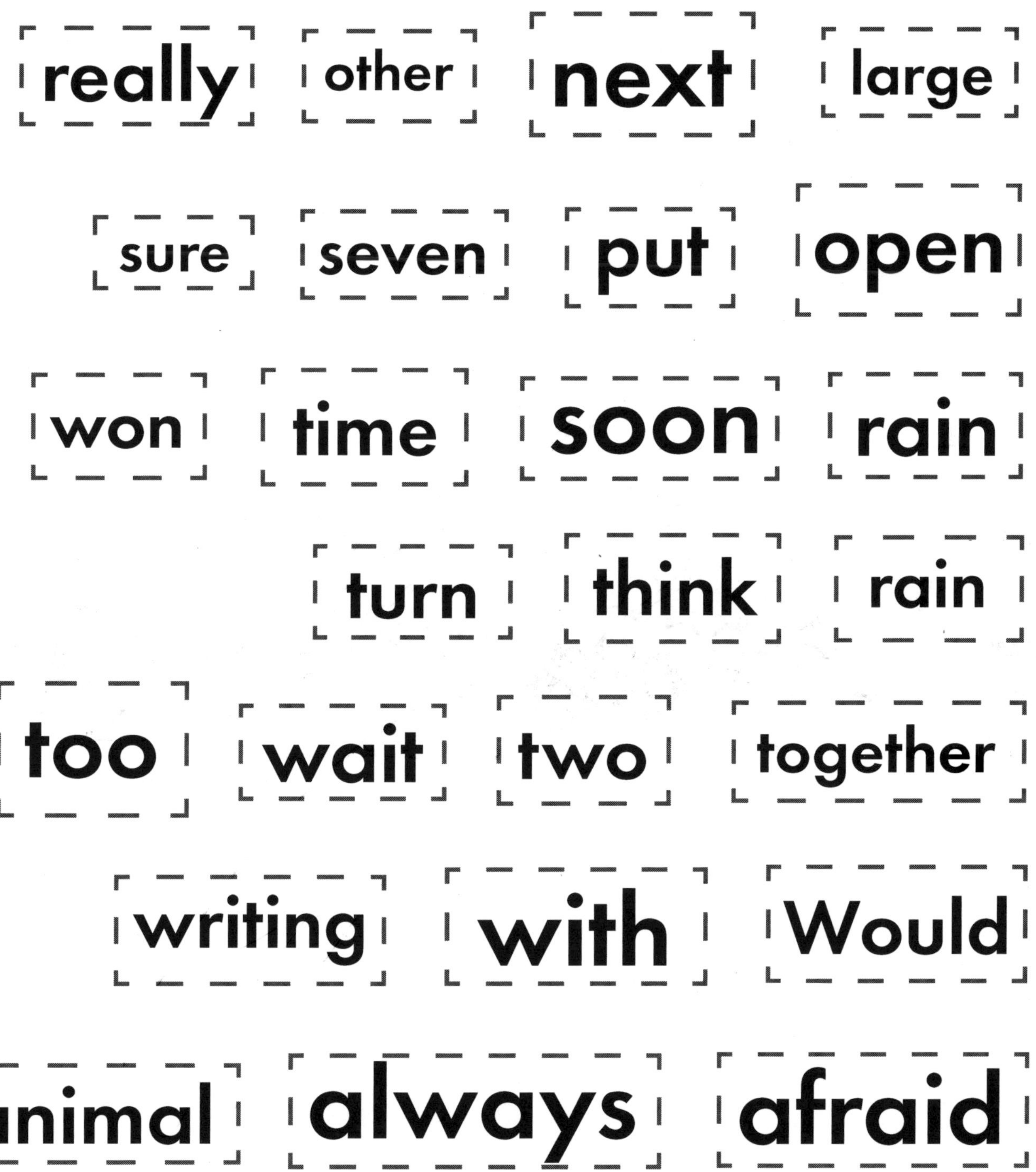

BRAIN
HUNTER

Instructions:

Locate the correct sight words and cut out the words carefully!
Paste the sight words into the corresponding pages.

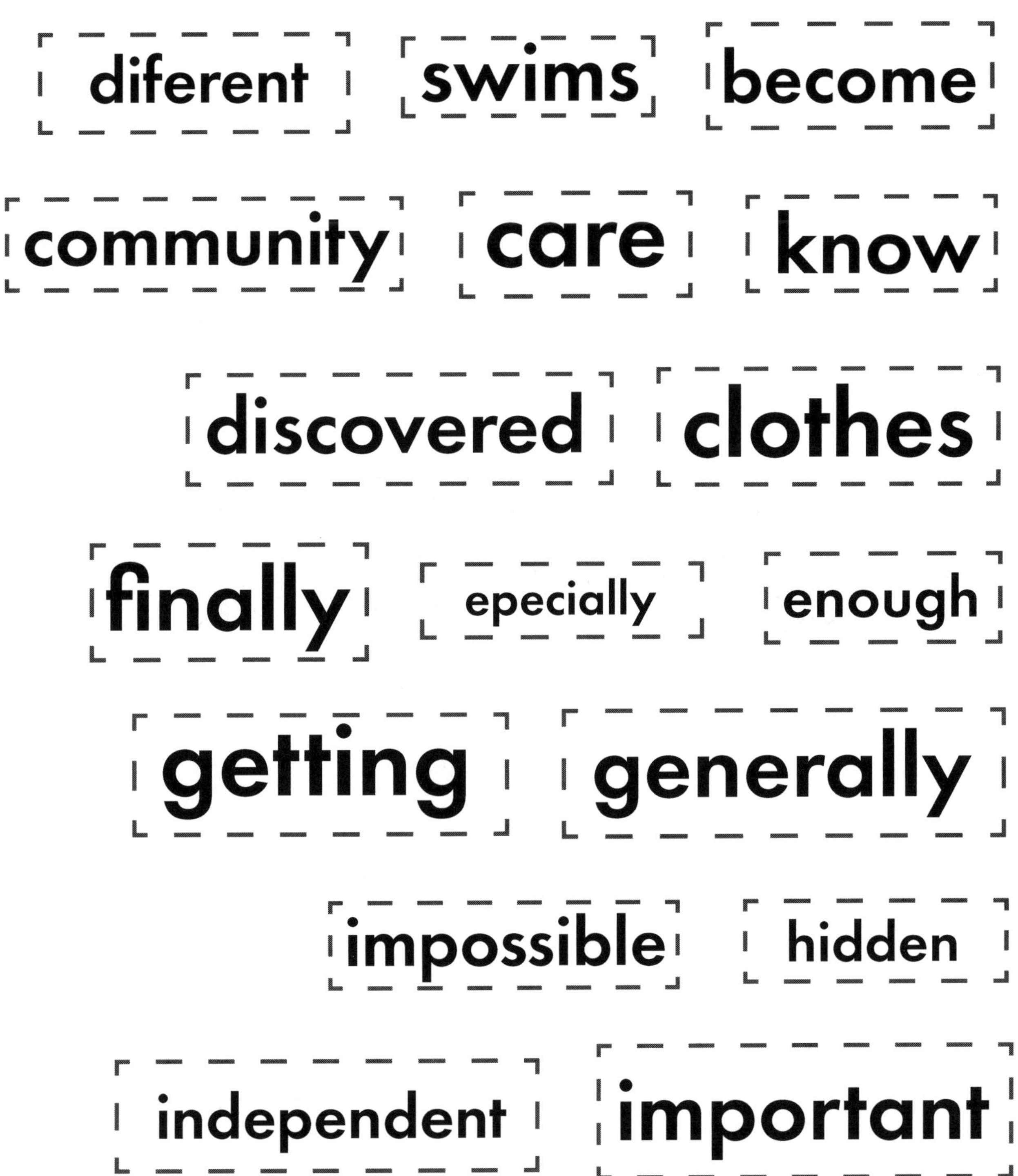

BRAIN
HUNTER

Instructions:
Locate the correct sight words and cut out the words carefully!
Paste the sight words into the corresponding pages.

Made in the USA
Columbia, SC
13 January 2019